Reuben G. Thwaites

Historic Waterways

Six hundred Miles of canoeing down the Rock, Fox and Wisconsin Rivers

Reuben G. Thwaites

Historic Waterways
Six hundred Miles of canoeing down the Rock, Fox and Wisconsin Rivers

ISBN/EAN: 9783337140939

Printed in Europe, USA, Canada, Australia, Japan

Cover: Foto ©ninafisch / pixelio.de

More available books at **www.hansebooks.com**

HISTORIC WATERWAYS

SIX HUNDRED MILES OF CANOEING

DOWN THE ROCK, FOX, AND

WISCONSIN RIVERS

BY

REUBEN GOLD THWAITES

SECRETARY OF THE STATE HISTORICAL SOCIETY OF WISCONSIN

Other roads do some violence to Nature, and bring the traveller to stare at her; but the river steals into the scenery it traverses without intrusion, silently creating and adorning it, and is free to come and go as the zephyr. — THOREAU; *A Week on the Concord and Merrimack Rivers.*

CHICAGO
A. C. McCLURG AND COMPANY
1888

This Little Volume

IS INSCRIBED BY THE AUTHOR

TO HIS WIFE,

HIS MESSMATE UPON TWO OF THE THREE VACATION
VOYAGES HEREIN RECORDED,
AND HIS FELLOW-VOYAGER DOWN THE RIVER
OF TIME.

PREFACE.

THERE is a generally accepted notion that a brief summer vacation, if at all obtainable in this busy life of ours, must be spent in a flight as far afield as time will allow; that the popular resorts in the mountains, by the seaside, or on the margins of the upper lakes must be sought for rest and enjoyment; that neighborhood surroundings should, in the mad rush for change of air and scene, be left behind. The result is that your average vacationist — if I may be allowed to coin a needed word — knows less of his own State than of any other, and is inattentive to the delights of nature which await inspection within the limits of his horizon.

But let him mount his bicycle, his saddle-horse, or his family carriage, and start out upon a gypsy tour of a week or two along the country roads, exploring the hills and plains and valleys of — say his congressional district; or, better by far, take his canoe, and with his best friend for a messmate explore the nearest river from source to mouth, and my word for it he will find novelty and fresh air enough to satisfy his utmost cravings; and when he comes to return to his counter, his desk, or his study, he will be conscious of having discovered charms in his own locality which he has in vain sought in the accustomed paths of the tourist.

This volume is the record of six hundred miles of canoeing experiences on historic waterways in Wisconsin and Illinois during the summer of 1887. There has been no attempt at exaggeration, to color its homely incidents, or to picture charms where none exist. It is intended to be a simple, truthful narrative of what was seen and done upon a series of novel outings through the heart of the Northwest. If it may induce others to undertake similar excursions, and thus increase the little navy of healthy and self-satisfied canoeists, the the object of the publication will have been attained.

I am under obligations to my friend, the Hon. Levi Alden, for valuable assistance in the revision of proof-sheets.

R. G. T.

MADISON, Wis., December, 1887.

CONTENTS.

	PAGE
Introduction	15
Table of Distances	26

The Rock River.

CHAPTER I.
The Winding Yahara 31

CHAPTER II.
Barbed-Wire Fences 48

CHAPTER III.
An Illinois Prairie Home 61

CHAPTER IV.
The Half-Way House 74

CHAPTER V.
Grand Detour Folks 86

CHAPTER VI.
An Ancient Mariner 103

CHAPTER VII.
Storm-Bound at Erie 117

CHAPTER VIII.
The Last Day Out 129

The Fox River (of Green Bay).

FIRST LETTER.
Smith's Island 143

SECOND LETTER.
From Packwaukee to Berlin 160

THIRD LETTER.
The Mascoutins 174

FOURTH LETTER.
The Land of the Winnebagoes 187

FIFTH LETTER.

LOCKED THROUGH 205

SIXTH LETTER.

THE BAY SETTLEMENT 218

The Wisconsin River.

CHAPTER I.
ALONE IN THE WILDERNESS 237

CHAPTER II.
THE LAST OF THE SACS 248

CHAPTER III.
A PANORAMIC VIEW 262

CHAPTER IV.
FLOATING THROUGH FAIRYLAND 275

CHAPTER V.
THE DISCOVERY OF THE MISSISSIPPI . . . 288

INDEX 295

INTRODUCTION.

HISTORIC WATERWAYS.

INTRODUCTION.

PROVIDED, reader, you have a goodly store of patience, stout muscles, a practiced fondness for the oars, a keen love of the picturesque and curious in nature, a capacity for remaining good-humored under the most adverse circumstances, together with a quiet love for that sort of gypsy life which we call "roughing it," canoeing may be safely recommended to you as one of the most delightful and healthful of outdoor recreations, as well as one of the cheapest.

The canoe need not be of birch-bark or canvas, or of the Rob Roy or Racine pattern. A plain, substantial, light, open clinker-build was what we used, — thirteen feet in extreme length, with three-and-a-half feet beam. It was easily portaged, held two persons comfortably with seventy-five pounds of baggage, and drew but five inches, — just enough to let us over the average shallows without bumping. It was serviceable, and stood the rough carries and innumerable bangs from sunken rocks and snags along its voyage of six hundred miles, without injury. It could carry a large sprit-sail, and, with an attachable keel, run close to the wind; while an awning, decided luxury on hot days, was readily hoisted on a pair of hoops attached to the gunwale on either side. But perhaps, where there are no portages necessary, an ordinary flat-bottomed river punt, built of three boards, would be as productive of good results, except as to speed, — and what matters speed upon such a tour of observation?

It is not necessary to go to the Maine lakes for canoeing purposes; or to skirt the gloomy wastes of Labrador, or descend the angry current of a mountain stream. Here, in the Mississippi basin, practically boundless opportunities present themselves, at our very doors, to glide through the heart of a fertile and picturesque land, to commune with Nature, to drink in her beauties, to view men and communities from a novel standpoint, to catch pictures of life and manners that will always live in one's memory. The traveler by rail has brief and imperfect glimpses of the landscape. The canoeist, from his lowly seat near the surface of the flood, sees the country practically as it was in pioneer days, in a state of unalloyed beauty. Each bend in the stream brings into view a new vista, and thus the bewitching scene changes as in a kaleidoscope. The people one meets, the variety of landscape one encounters, the simple adventures of the day, the sensation of being an explorer, the fresh air and simple diet, combined with that spirit of calm contentedness which overcomes the happy voyager who casts loose from care, are the never-failing attractions of such a trip.

To those would-be canoeists who are fond of the romantic history of our great West, as well as of delightful scenery, the Fox (of Green Bay), the Rock, and the Wisconsin, each with its sharply distinctive features, will be found among the most interesting of our neighborhood rivers. And this record of recent voyages upon them is, I think, fairly representative of what sights and experiences await the boatman upon any of the streams of similar importance in the vast and well-watered region of the upper Mississippi valley.

Of the three, the Rock river route, through

the great prairies of Illinois, perhaps presents the greatest variety of **life and scenery**. The Rock has practically two heads: the smaller, in a rustic stream flowing from the north into swamp-girted Lake Koshkonong; the larger, in the four lakes at Madison, the charming **capital of** Wisconsin, which empty their waters into the Avon-like Catfish or Yahara, which in turn pours into the Rock a short distance below the Koshkonong lake. Our course was from Madison **almost to** the mouth of the Rock, near Rock Island, 267 miles of paddling, **as** the river winds.

The student of history finds the Rock interesting to him because of its associations with the Black Hawk war of 1832. When the famous Sac warrior "invaded" Illinois, his path of progress was up the south bank of that stream. At Prophetstown lived his evil genius, the crafty White Cloud, and here the Hawk held council with the Pottawattomies, who, **under** good Shaubena's influence, rejected **the** war pipe. Dixon is famous as **the** site of the pioneer ferry over the Rock, on the line of what **was** the principal land highway between Chicago and southern Wisconsin and the Galena mines for a protracted period in each year. Here, many a notable party of explorers, military officials, miners, and traders have rendezvoused in the olden time. Here was a rallying-point in 1832, as well, when Lincoln was a raw-boned militia-man in a scouting corps, and Robert Anderson, of Fort Sumter fame, Zachary Taylor, and Jefferson Davis were of the regular army under bluff old Atkinson. A grove at the mouth of Stillman's Creek, a Rock River tributary, near Byron, is the scene of the actual outbreak of the war. The forest where Black Hawk camped with the white-loving Pottawattomies is practically unchanged, and the open, rolling prairie to the south — on which Stillman's horsemen acted at first so treacherously, and afterwards as arrant cowards — is still there, a broad pasture-land miles in length, along the river. The contemporaneous descriptions of the " battle " field are readily recognizable to-day. Above, as far as Lake Koshkonong, the river banks are fraught with interest; for along them the soldiery followed up the Sac trail, like bloodhounds, and held many an unsatisfactory parley with the double-faced Winnebagoes.

Rock River scenery combines the rustic, the romantic, and the picturesque, — prairies, meadows, ravines, swamps, mountainous bluffs, eroded palisades, wide stretches of densely wooded bottoms, heavy upland forests, shallows, spits, and rapids. Birds and flowers, and uncommon plants and vines, delight the naturalist and the botanist. The many thriving manufacturing cities, — such as Stoughton, Janesville, Beloit, Rockford, Rockton, Dixon, Sterling, and Oregon, — furnish an abundance of sight-seeing. The small villages — some of them odd, out-of-the-way places, of rare types — are worthy of study to the curious in economics and human nature. The farmers are of many types; the fishermen one is thrown into daily communion with are a class unto themselves; while millers, bridge-tenders, boat-renters, and others whose callings are along-shore, present a variety of humanity interesting and instructive. The twenty-odd mill-dam portages, each having difficulties and incidents of its own, are well calculated to vary the monotony of the voyage; there are more or less dangers connected with some of the mill-races, while the lookout for snags, bowlders and shallows must be continuous, sharpening the senses of sight and sound; for a tip-over or the utter demolition of the craft may readily follow carelessness in this direction. The islands in the Rock are numerous, many of them being several miles in length, and nearly all heavily wooded. These frequent divisions of the channel often give rise to much perplexity; for the ordinary summer stage of water is so low that a loaded canoe drawing five inches of water is liable to be stranded in the channel apparently most available.

The Fox and Wisconsin rivers — the former, from Portage to Green Bay, the latter from Portage to Prairie du Chien — form a water highway that has been in use by white men for two and a half centuries. In 1634, Jean Nicolet, the first explorer of the Northwest, passed up the Fox River, to about Berlin, and then went southward to visit the Illinois. In the month of June, 1673, Joliet and Marquette made their famous tour over the interlocked watercourse and discovered the Mississippi River. After they had shown the way, a tide of travel set in over these twin streams, between the Great Lakes and the great river, — a motley procession of Jesuit missionaries, explorers, traders, trappers, soldiers and pioneers. New England was in its infancy when the Fox and Wisconsin became an established highway for enterprising canoeists.

Since the advent of the railway era this historic channel of communication has fallen into disuse. The general government has spent an immense sum in endeavoring to render it navigable for the vessels in vogue to-day, but the result, as a whole, is a failure. There is no navigation on the Fox worthy of mention, above Berlin, and even that below is insignificant and intermittent. On the Wisconsin there is none at all, except for skiffs and an occasional lumber-raft.

The canoeist of to-day, therefore, will find solitude and shallows enough on either river. But he can float, if historically inclined, through the dusky shadows of the past, for every turn of the bank has its story, and there is romance enough to stock a volume.

The upper Fox is rather monotonous. The river twists and turns through enormous widespreads, grown up with wild rice and flecked with water-fowl. These widespreads occasionally free themselves of vegetable growth and become lakes, like the Buffalo, the Puckawa, and the Poygan. There is, however, much of interest to the student in natural history; while such towns as Montello, Princeton, Berlin, Omro, Winneconne, and Oshkosh are worthy of visitation. Lake Winnebago is a notable inland sea, and the canoeist feels fairly lost, in his little cockle shell, bobbing about over its great waves. The lower Fox runs between high, noble banks, and with frequent rapids, past Neenah,

Menasha, Appleton, and other busy manufacturing cities, down to Green Bay, hoary with age and classic in her shanty ruins.

The Wisconsin River is the most picturesque of the three. Probably the best route is from the head of the Dells to the mouth ; but the run from Portage to the mouth is the one which has the merit of antiquity, and is certainly a long enough jaunt to satisfy the average tourist. It is a wide, gloomy, mountain-girt valley, with great sand-bars and thickly-wooded morasses. Settlement is slight. Portage, Prairie du Sac, Sauk City, and Muscoda are the principal towns. The few villages are generally from a mile to three miles back, at the foot of the bluffs, out of the way of the flood, and the river appears to be but little used. It is an ideal sketching-ground. The canoeist with a camera will find occupation enough in taking views of his surroundings ; perplexity as to what to choose amid such a crowd of charming scenes, will be his only difficulty.

Some suggestions to those who may wish to undertake these or similar river trips may be advisable. Traveling alone will be found too dreary. None but a hermit could enjoy those long stretches of waterway, where one may float for a day without seeing man or animal on the forest-bounded shores, and where the oppression of solitude is felt with such force that it requires but a slight stretch of imagination to carry one's self back in thought and feeling to the days when the black-robed members of the Company of Jesus first penetrated the gloomy wilderness. Upon the size of the party should depend the character of the preparations. If the plan is to spend the nights at farmhouses or village taverns, then a party of two will be as large as can secure comfortable quarters,— especially at a farmhouse, where but one spare bed can usually be found, while many are the country inns where the accommodations are equally limited. If it is intended to tent on the banks, then the party should be larger; for two persons unused to this experience would find it exceedingly lonesome after nightfall, when visions of river tramps, dissolute fishermen, and inquisitive hogs and bulls, pass in review, and the weakness of the little camp against such formidable odds comes to be fully recognized. Often, too, the camping-places are few and far between, and may involve a carry of luggage to higher lands beyond; on such occasions, the more assistance the merrier. But whatever the preparations for the night and breakfast, the mess-box must be relied upon for dinners and suppers, for there is no dining-car to be taken on along these water highways, and eating-stations are unknown.. Unless there are several towns on the route, of over one thousand inhabitants, it would be well to carry sufficient provisions of a simple sort for the entire trip, for supplies are difficult to obtain at small villages, and the quality is apt to be poor. Farmhouses can generally be depended on for eggs, butter, and milk,— nothing more. For drinking-water, obtainable from farm-wells, carry an army canteen, if you can get one; if not, a stone jug will do. The river water is useful only for floating the canoe, and the offices of the bath. As to personal baggage, fly very light, as a draught of over six inches would at times work an estoppel to your progress on any of the three streams mentioned. In shipping your boat to any point at which you wish to embark upon a river, allow two or three days for freight-train delays.

Be prepared to find canoeing a rough sport. There is plenty of hard work about it, a good deal of sunburn and blister. You will be obliged to wear your old clothes, and may not be overpleased to meet critical friends in the river towns you visit. But if you have the true spirit of the canoeist, you **will win** for your pains an abundance of good air, good scenery, wholesome exercise, sound sleep, and **and something** to think about all your life.

TABLE OF DISTANCES.—TOTAL, 607 MILES.

THE ROCK RIVER.

	MILES.
Madison to Stoughton	22
Stoughton to Janesville	40
Janesville to Beloit	18
Beloit to Rockford	40
Rockford to Byron	18
Byron to Oregon	15
Oregon to Dixon	31
Dixon to Sterling	20
Sterling to Como	9
Como to Lyndon	14
Lyndon to Prophetstown	5
Prophetstown to Erie Ferry	10
Erie Ferry to Coloma	25
Coloma to mouth of river	14
Mouth of river to Rock Island (up Mississippi River)	6
Total	287

THE FOX RIVER (OF GREEN BAY).

	MILES.
Portage to Packwaukee	25
Packwaukee to Montello	7
Montello to Marquette	11

Introduction. 27

	MILES.
Marquette to Princeton	18
Princeton to Berlin	20
Berlin to Omro	18
Omro to Oshkosh	22
Oshkosh to Neenah	20
Neenah to **Appleton**	7
Appleton to **Kaukauna**	7
Kaukauna to **Green Bay**	20
Total	175

THE WISCONSIN RIVER.

	MILES.
Portage to Merrimac	20
Merrimac to Prairie du Sac	10
Prairie du Sac to Arena Ferry	15
Arena Ferry to Helena	8
Helena **to Lone** Rock **Bridge**	14
Lone Rock Bridge **to** Muscoda	18
Muscoda to Port **Andrew**	9
Port Andrew to Boscobel	10
Boscobel to Boydtown	10
Boydtown to Wauzeka **(on** Kickapoo)	7
Wauzeka to Wright's Ferry	10
Wright's Ferry to Bridgeport	4
Bridgeport to mouth of river	7
Mouth of river to Prairie du Chien (up Mississippi River)	5
Total	145

NOTE. — The above table of distances **by water** is based upon the most reliable local estimates, verified, as far as practicable, by official surveys.

THE ROCK RIVER.

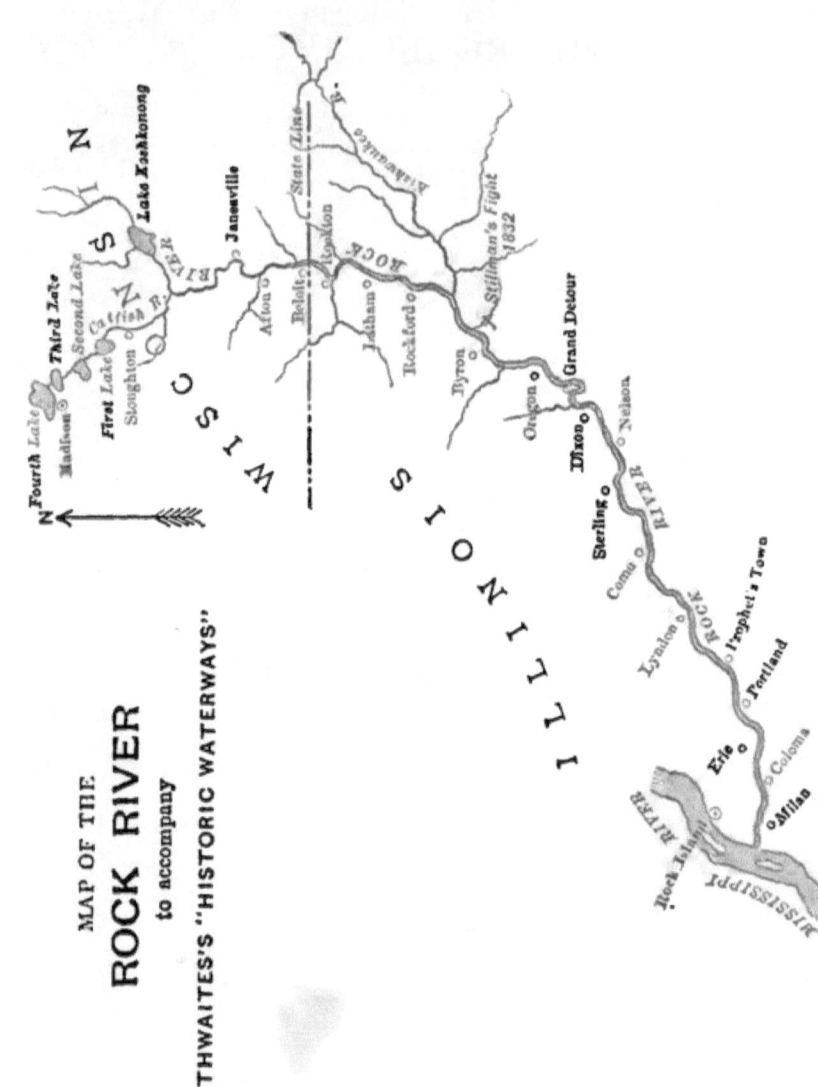

THE ROCK RIVER.

CHAPTER I.

THE WINDING YAHARA.

IT was a quarter to twelve, Monday morning, the 23d of May, 1887, when we took seats in our canoe at our own landing-stage on Third Lake, at Madison, spread an awning over two hoops, as on a Chinese house-boat, pushed off, waved farewell to a little group of curious friends, and started on our way to explore the Rock River of Illinois. W—— wielded the paddle astern, while I took the oars amidships. Despite the one hundred pounds of baggage and the warmth emitted by the glowing sun, — for the season was unusually advanced, — we made excellent speed, as we well had need in order to reach the mouth, a distance of two hundred and eighty miles as the sinuous river runs, in the seven days we had allotted to the task.

It was a delightful run across the southern arm of the lake. There was a light breeze aft, which gave a graceful upward curvature to our low-set awning. The great elms and lindens at charming Lakeside — the home of the Wisconsin Chautauqua — droop over the bowlder-studded banks, their masses of greenery almost sweeping the water. Down in the deep, cool shadows groups of bass and pickerel and perch lazily swish; swarms of "crazy bugs" ceaselessly swirl around and around, with no apparent object in life but this rhythmic motion, by which they wrinkle the mirror-like surface into concentric circles. Through occasional openings in the dense fringe of pendent boughs, glimpses can be had of park-like glades, studded with columnar oaks, and stretching upward to hazel-grown knolls, which rise in irregular succession beyond the bank. From the thickets comes the fussy chatter of thrushes and cat-birds, calling to their young or gossiping with the orioles, the robins, jays, and red-breasted grosbeaks, who warble and twitter and scream and trill from more lofty heights.

A quarter of an hour sent us spinning across the mouth of Turvill's Bay. At Ott's

Farm, just beyond, the bank rises with sheer ascent, in layers of crumbly sandstone, a dozen feet above the water's level. Close-cropped woodlawn pastures gently slope upward to storm-wracked orchards, and long, dark windbreaks of funereal spruce. Flocks of sheep, fresh from the shearing, trot along the banks, winding in and out between the trees, keeping us company on our way, — their bleating lambs following at a lope, — now and then stopping, in their eager, fearful curiosity, to view our craft, and assuming picturesque attitudes, worthy subjects for a painter's art.

A long, hard pull through close-grown patches of reeds and lily-pads, encumbered by thick masses of green scum, brought us to the outlet of the lake and the head of that section of the Catfish River which is the medium through which Third Lake pours its overflow into Second. The four lakes of Madison are connected by the Catfish, the chief Wisconsin tributary of the Rock. Upon the map this relationship reminds one of beads strung upon a thread.

As the result of a protracted drought, the water in the little stream was low, and great clumps of aquatic weeds came very close to the surface, threatening, later in the season, an almost complete stoppage to navigation. But the effect of the current was at once perceptible. It was as if an additional rower had been taken on. The river, the open stream of which is some three rods wide at this point, winds like a serpent between broad marshes, which must at no far distant period in the past have been wholly submerged, thus prolonging the three upper lakes into a continuous sheet of water. From a half-mile to a mile back, on either side, there are low ridges, doubtless the ancient shores of a narrow lake that was probably thirty or forty miles in length. In high water, even now, the marshes are converted into widespreads, where the dense tangle of wild rice, reeds, and rushes does not wholly prevent canoe navigation; while little mud-bottomed lakes, a quarter of a mile or so in diameter, are frequently met with at all stages. In places, the river, during a drought, has a depth of not over eighteen inches. In such stretches, the current moves swiftly over hard bottoms strewn with gravel and the whitened sepulchres of snails and clams. In the widespreads, the progress is sluggish, the vegetable growth so crowding in upon the stream as to leave but a narrow and devious channel, requiring skill to pilot through; for in these labyrinthian turn-ings one is quite liable, if not closely watching the lazy flood, to push into some vexatious cul-de-sac, many rods in length, and be obliged to retrace, with the danger of mistaking a branch for the main channel.

In the depths of the tall reeds motherly mud-hens are clucking, while their mates squat in the open water, in meditative groups, rising with a prolonged splash and a whirr as the canoe approaches within gunshot. Secluded among the rushes and cat-tails, nestled down in little clumps of stubble, are hundreds of the cup-shaped nests of the red-winged blackbird, or American starling; the females, in modest brown, take a rather pensive view of life, administering to the wants of their young; while the bright-hued, talkative males, perched on swaying stalks, fairly make the air hum with their cheery trills.

Water-lilies abound everywhere. The blossoms of the yellow variety (nuphar advena) are here and there bursting in select groups, but as a rule the buds are still below the surface. In the mud lakes, the bottom is seen through the crystal water to be thickly studded with great rosettes, two and three feet in diameter, of corrugated ovate leaves, of golden russet shade, out of which are shot upward brilliant green stalks, some bearing arrow-shaped leaves, and others crowned with the tight-wrapped buds that will soon open upon the water level into saffron-hued flowers. The plate-like leaves of the white variety (nymphæa tuberosa) already dot the surface, but the buds are not yet visible. Anchored by delicate stems to the creeping root-stalks, buried in the mud below, the leaves, when first emerging, are of a rich golden brown, but they are soon frayed by the waves, and soiled and eaten by myriads of water-bugs, slugs, and spiders, who make their homes on these floating islands. Pluck a leaf, and the many-legged spiders, the roving buccaneers of these miniature seas, stalk off at high speed, while the slugs and leeches, in a spirit of stubborn patriotism, prefer meeting death upon their native heath to politic emigration.

By one o'clock we had reached the railway bridge at the head of Second Lake. Upon the trestlework were perched three boys and a man, fishing. They had that listless air and unkempt appearance which are so characteristic of the little groups of humanity often to be found on a fair day angling from piers, bridges, and railway embankments. Men who imagine the world is allied against them will loll away a dozen hours a day, throughout an entire summer season, sitting on the sun-heated girders of an iron bridge; yet they would strike against any system in the work-a-day world which compelled them to labor more than eight hours for ten hours' pay. In going down a long stretch of water highway, one comes to believe that about one-quarter of the inhabitants, especially of the villages, spend their time chiefly in fishing. On a canoe voyage, the bridge fishermen and the birds are the classes of animated nature most frequently met with, the former presenting perhaps the most unique and varied specimens. There are fishermen and fishermen. I never could fancy Izaak Walton dangling his legs from a railroad bridge, soaking a worm at the end of a length of store twine, vainly hoping, as the hours went listlessly by, that a stray sucker or a diminutive catfish would pull the bob under and score a victory for patience. Now the use of a boat lifts this sort of thing to the dignity of a sport.

Second Lake is about three miles long by a mile in breadth. The shores are here and there marshy; but as a rule they are of good, firm land with occasional rocky bluffs from a dozen to twenty feet high, rising sheer from a narrow beach of gravel. As we crossed over to gain the lower Catfish, a calm prevailed for the most part, and the awning was a decided comfort. Now and then, however, a delightful puff came ruffling the water astern, swelling our canvas roof and noticeably helping us along. Light cloudage, blown swiftly before upper aerial currents, occasionally obscured the sun, — black, gray, and white cumuli fantastically shaped and commingled, while through jagged and rapidly shifting gaps was to be seen with vivid effect, the deep blue ether beyond.

The bluffs and glades are well wooded. The former have escarpments of yellow clay and grayish sand and gravel; here and there have been landslides, where great trees have fallen with the débris and maintain but a slender hold amid their new surroundings, leaning far out over the water, easy victims for the next tornado. One monarch of the woods had been thus precipitated into the flood; on one side, its trunk and giant branches were water-soaked and slimy, while those above were dead and whitened by storm. As we approached, scores of turtles, sunning themselves on the unsubmerged portion, suddenly ducked their heads and slid off their perches amid a general splash, to hidden grottos below; while a solitary king-fisher from his vantage height on an upper bough hurriedly rose, and screamed indignance at our rude entry upon his preserve.

A farmer's lad sitting squat upon his haunches on the beach, and another, leaning over a pasture-fence, holding his head between his hands, exhibited lamb-like curiosity at the awning-decked canoe, as it glided past their bank. Through openings in the forest, we caught glimpses of rolling upland pastures, with sod close-cropped and smooth as a well-kept lawn; of gray-blue fields, recently seeded; of farmhouses, spacious barns, tobacco-curing sheds,—for this is the heart of the Wisconsin tobacco region,—and those inevitable signs of rural prosperity, windmills, spinning around by spurts, obedient to the breath of the intermittent May-day zephyr; while little bays opened up, on the most distant shore, enchanting vistas of blue-misted ridges.

At last, after a dreamy pull of two miles from the lake-head, we rounded a bold headland of some thirty feet in height, and entered Catfish Bay. Ice-pushed bowlders strew the shore, which is here a gentle meadow slope, based by a gravel beach. A herd of cattle are contentedly browsing, their movements attuned to a symphony of cow-bells dangling from the necks of the leaders. The scene is pre-eminently peaceful.

The Catfish connecting Second Lake with First, has two entrances, a small flat willow island dividing them. Through the eastern channel, which is the deepest, the current goes down with a rush, the obstruction offered by numerous bowlders churning it into noisy rapids; but the water tames down within a few rods, and the canoe comes gayly gliding into the united stream, which now has a placid current of two miles per hour,—quite fast enough for canoeing purposes. This section of the Catfish is much more picturesque than the preceding; the shores are firmer; the parallel ridges sometimes closely shut it in, and the stream, here four or five rods wide, takes upon itself the characteristics of the conventional river. The weed and vine grown banks are oftentimes twenty feet in height, with as sharp an ascent as can be comfortably climbed; and the swift-rushing water is sometimes fringed with sumachs, elders, and hazel brush, with here and there willows, maples, lindens, and oaks. Occasionally the river apparently ends at the base of a steep, earthy bluff; but when that is reached there is a sudden swerve to the right or left, with another vista of banks,—sometimes wood-grown to the water's edge, again with openings revealing purplish-brown fields, neatly harrowed, stretching up to some commanding, forest-crowned hill-top. The blossoms of the wild grape burden the air with sweet scent ; on the deep-shaded banks, amid stones and cool mosses, the red and yellow columbine gracefully nods ; the mandrake, with its glossy green leaves, grows with tropical luxuriance ; more in the open, appears in great profusion, the old maid's nightcap, in purplish roseate hue ; the sheep-berry shrub is decked in masses of white blossoms ; the hawthorn flower is detected by its sickly-sweet scent, and here and there are luxuriously-flowered locusts, specimens that have escaped from cultivation to take up their homes in this botanical wilderness.

There are charming rustic pictures at every turn, — sleek herds of cattle, droves of fat hogs, flocks of sheep that have but recently doffed their winter suits, well-tended fields, trim-looking wire fences, neat farm-houses where rows of milkpans glisten upon sunny drying-benches, farmers and farmers' boys riding aristocratic-looking sulky drags and cultivators, — everywhere an air of agricultural luxuriance, rather emphasized by occasional log-houses, which repose as honored relics by the side of their pretentious successors, sharply contrasting the wide differences between pioneer life and that of to-day.

The marshes **are few**; and they in this dry season are luxuriant with coarse, glossy wild grass, — the only hay-crop **the far**mer will have this year, — and dotted with clumps of dead willow-trees, which present a ghostly appearance, waving their white, scarred limbs in the freshening breeze. The most beautiful spot on this section of the Catfish is a point some eight miles above Stoughton. The verdure-clad banks are high and steep. A lanky Norwegian farmer came down an angling path with a pail-yoke over his shoulders to get washing-water for his "woman," and told us that when this country was sparsely settled, a third of a century ago, there was a mill-dam here. That was the day when the possession **of** water-power meant more than it does in this age of steam and rapid transit, — the day when every mill-site was supposed to be a nucleus around which a prosperous village must necessarily grow in due time. Nothing now remains as a relic of this particular fond hope but great hollows in either bank, where the clay for dam-making purposes has been scooped out, and a few rotten piles, having a slender hold upon the bottom, against which drift-wood has lodged, forming a home for turtles and clumps of semi-aquatic grasses. W—— avers, in a spirit of enthusiasm, that the Catfish between Second and First Lakes is quite similar in parts to the immortal Avon, upon which Shakespeare canoed in the long-ago. If she is right, then indeed are the charms of Avon worthy the praise of the Muses. If the Catfish of to-day is ever to go down to posterity on the wings of poesy, however, I would wish that it might be with the more euphonious title of "Yahara,"—the original Winnebago name. The map-maker who first dropped the liquid "Yahara" for the rasping "Catfish" had no soul for music.

Darting under a quaint rustic foot-bridge made of rough poles, which on its high trestles stalks over a wide expanse of reedy bog like a giant "stick-bug," we emerged into First Lake. The eastern shore, which we skirted, is a wide, sandy beach, backed by meadows. The opposite banks, two or three miles away, present more picturesque outlines. A stately wild swan kept us company for over a mile, just out of musket-shot, and finally took advantage of a patch of rushes to stop and hide. A small sandstone quarry on the southeast shore, with a lone worker, attracted our attention. There was not a human habitation in sight, and it seemed odd to see a solitary man engaged in such labor apparently so far removed from the highways of commerce. The quarryman stuck his crowbar in a crack horizontally, to serve as a seat, and filled his pipe as we approached. We hailed him with inquiries, from the stone pier jutting into the lake at the foot of the bluff into which he was burrowing. He replied from his lofty perch, in rich Norsk brogue, that he shipped stone by barge to Stoughton, and good-humoredly added, as he struck a match and lit his bowl of weed, that he thought himself altogether too good company to ever get lonesome. We left the philosopher to enjoy his pipe in peace, and passed on around the headland.

An iron railway bridge, shut in with high sides, and painted a dullish red, spans the Lower Catfish at the outlet of First Lake. A country boy, with face as dirty as it was solemn, stood in artistic rags at the base of an arch, fishing with a bit of hop-twine tied to the end of a lath; from a mass of sedge just behind him a hoarse cry arose at short intervals.

"Hi, Johnny, what's that making the noise?"

"Bird!" sententiously responded the stoic

youth. He looked as though he had been bored with a silly question, and kept his eyes on his task.

"What kind of a bird, Johnny?"

"D' no!" rather raspishly. He evidently thought he was being guyed.

We ran the nose of the canoe into the reeds. There was a splash, a wild cry of alarm, and up flew a great bittern. Circling about until we had passed on, it then drifted down to its former location near the uninquiring lad, — where doubtless it had a nest of young, and had been disturbed in the midst of a lecture on domestic discipline.

Wide marshes again appear on either side of the stream. There are great and small bitterns at every view; plovers daintily picking their way over the open bogs, greedily feeding on countless snails; wild ducks in plenty, patiently waiting in the secluded bayous for the development of their young; yellow-headed troopials flitting freely about, uttering a choking, gulping cry; while the pert little wren, with his smart cock-tail, views the varied scene from his perch on a lofty rush, jealously keeping watch and ward over his ball-like castle, with its secret gate, hung among the reeds below.

But interspersing the marshes there are

often stretches of firm bank and delightfully
varied glimpses of hillside and wood. Three
miles above Stoughton, we stopped for supper
at the edge of a glade, near a quaint old bridge.
While seated on the smooth sward, beside
our little spread, there came a vigorous rustling among the branches of the trees that
overhang the country road which winds down
the opposite slope to the water's edge to take
advantage of the crossing. A gypsy wagon,
with a high, rounded, oil-cloth top soon
emerged from the forest, and was seen to
have been the cause of the disturbance.
Halting at one side of the highway, three
men and a boy jumped out, unhitched the
horses at the pole and the jockeying stock at
the tail-board, and led them down to water.
Two women meanwhile set about getting supper, and preparations were made for a night
camp. We confessed to a touch of sympathy
with our new neighbors on the other shore,
for we felt as though gypsying ourselves. The
hoop awning on the canoe certainly had the
general characteristics of a gypsy-wagon
top; we knew not and cared not where night
might overtake us; we were dependent on
the country for our provender; were at the
mercy of wind, weather, and the peculiarities
of our chosen highway; and had deliberately

turned our backs on home for a season of untrammeled communion with nature.

It was during a golden sunset that, pushing on through a great widespread, through which the channel doubles and twists like a scotched snake, we came in sight of the little city of Stoughton. First, the water-works tower rises above the mass of trees which embower the settlement. Then, on nearer approach, through rifts in the woodland we catch glimpses of some of the best outlying residences, most of them pretty, with well-kept grounds. Then come the church-spires, the ice-houses, the barge-dock, and with a spurt we sweep alongside the foundry of Mandt's wagon-works. Depositing our oars, paddle, blankets, and supplies in the office, the canoe was pulled up on the grass and padlocked to a stake. The street lamps were lighting as we registered at the inn.

Stoughton has about two thousand inhabitants. A walk about town in the evening, revealed a number of bright, busy shops, chiefly kept by Norwegians, who predominate in this region. Nearly every street appears to end in one of Mandt's numerous factory yards, and the wagon-making magnate seems to control pretty much the entire river front here.

CHAPTER II.

BARBED-WIRE FENCES.

WE were off in the morning, after an early breakfast at the Stoughton inn. Our host kindly sent down his porter to help us over the mill-dam, — our first and easiest portage, and one of the few in which we received assistance of any kind. Below this, as below all of the dams on the river, there are broad shallows. The water in the stream, being at a low stage, is mainly absorbed in the mill-race, and the apron spreads the slight overflow evenly over the width of the bed, so that there is left a wide expanse of gravel and rocks below the chute, which is not covered sufficiently deep for navigating even our little craft, drawing but five inches when fully loaded. We soon grounded on the shallows and I was obliged to get out and tow the lightened boat to the tail of the race, where deeper water was henceforth assured. This experience became quite familiar before the end of the trip. I had fortunately brought a pair of rubbers in my satchel, and found them invaluable as wading-shoes, where the river bottom is strewn with sharp gravel and slimy round-heads.

Below Stoughton the river winds along in most graceful curves, for the most part between banks from six to twenty feet high, with occasional pocket-marshes, in which the skunk-cabbage luxuriates. The stream is often thickly studded with lily-pads, which the wind, blowing fresh astern, frequently ruffles so as to give the appearance of rapids ahead, inducing caution where none is necessary. But every half-mile or so there are genuine little rapids, some of them requiring care to successfully shoot; in low water the canoe goes bumping along over the small moss-grown rocks, and now and then plumps solidly on a big one; when the stream is turbid, — as often happens below a pasture, where the cattle stir up the bank mud, — the danger of being overturned by scarcely submerged bowlders is imminent.

There are some decidedly romantic spots, where little densely-wooded and grape-tangled glens run off at right angles, leading up to the bases of commanding hillocks, which they drain; or where the noisy little river, five or six rods wide, goes swishing around the foot of a precipitous, bush-grown bluff. It is noticeable that in such beauty-spots as these are generally to be found poverty-stricken cabins, the homes of small fishermen and hunters; while the more generous farm-houses seek the fertile but prosaic openings.

All of a sudden, around a lovely bend, a barbed-wire fence of four strands savagely disputed the passage. A vigorous back-water stroke alone saved us from going full tilt into the bayonets of the enemy. We landed, and there was a council of war. As every stream in Wisconsin capable of floating a saw-log is "navigable" in the eye of the law, it is plain that this obstruction is an illegal one. Being an illegal fence, it follows that any canoeist is entitled to clip the wires, if he does not care to stop and prosecute the fencers for barring his way. The object of the structure is to prevent cattle from walking around through the shallow river into neighboring pastures. Along the upper Catfish, where boating is more frequently indulged in, farmers accomplish the same object by fencing in a few feet of the stream parallel with the shore. But below Stoughton, where canoeing is seldom practiced, the cattle-owners run their

fences directly across the river as a measure of economy. Taking into consideration the fact that the lower Catfish is seldom used as a highway, we concluded that we would be charitable and leave the fences intact, getting under or over them as best we might. I am afraid that had we known that twenty-one of these formidable barriers were before us, the council would not have agreed on so conciliatory a campaign.

Having taken in our awning and disposed of our baggage amidships, so that nothing remained above the gunwale, W——, kneeling, took the oars astern, while I knelt in the bow with the paddle borne like a battering-ram. Pushing off into the channel we bore down on the centre of the works, which were strong and thickly-posted, with wires drawn as tight as a drum-string. Catching the lower strand midway between two posts, on the blade end of the paddle, the speed of the canoe **was** checked. Then, seizing that strand with my right hand, so that the thick-strewn barbs came between my fingers, I forced it up to the second strand, and held the two rigidly together, thus making a slight arch. The canoe being crowded down into the water by sheer exercise of muscle, I crouched low in the bow, at the same time forcing the canoe under and forward through the arch. When half-way through, W—— was able similarly to clutch the wires, and perform the same office for the stern. This operation, ungraceful but effective, was frequently repeated during the day. When the current is swift and the wind fresh a special exertion is necessary on the part of the stern oar to keep the craft at right angles with the fence, — the tendency being, as soon as the bow is snubbed, to drift alongside and become entangled in the wires, with the danger of being either badly scratched or upset. It is with a feeling of no slight relief that a canoeist emerges from a tussle with a barbed-wire fence; and if hands, clothing, and boat have escaped without a scratch, he may consider himself fortunate, indeed. Before the day was through, when our twenty-one fences had been conquered without any serious accident, it was unanimously voted that the exercise was not to be recommended to those weak in muscle or patience.

Eight miles below Stoughton is Dunkirk. There is a neat frame grist-mill there; and up a gentle slope to the right are four or five weather-beaten farm-houses, in the corners of the cross-roads. It was an easy portage at the dam. After pushing through the shallows below with some difficulty, we ran in under the shadow of a substantial wagon-bridge, and beached. Going up to the corners, we filled the canteen with ice-cold water from a moss-grown well, and interviewed the patriarchal miller, who assured us that "nigh onter a dozen year ago, Dunkirk had a bigger show for growin' than Stoughton, but the railroad went 'round us."

A few miles down stream and we come to Stebbinsville. The water is backset by a mill-dam for two miles, forming a small lake. The course now changing, the wind came dead ahead, and we rowed down to the dam in a rolling sea, with much exertion. The river is six rods wide here, flowing between smooth, well-rounded, grass-grown banks, from fifteen to thirty feet in height, the fields on either side sloping up to wood-crowned ridges. There are a mill and two houses at Stebbinsville, and the country round about has a prosperous appearance. A tall, pleasant-spoken young miller came across the road-bridge and talked to us about the crops and the river, while we made a comfortable portage of five rods, up the grassy bank and through a close-cropped pasture, down to a sequestered little bay at the tail of an abandoned race, where the spray of the falls spattered us as we reloaded. We pushed off, with the joint opinion that Stebbinsville was a charming little place, with ideal riverside homes, that would be utterly spoiled by building the city on its site which the young man said his father had always hoped would be established there. A quarter of a mile below, around the bend, is a disused mill, thirty feet up, on the right bank. There is a suspended platform over a ravine, to one side of the building, and upon its handrail leaned two dusty millers, who had doubtless hastened across from the upper mill, to watch the progress down the little rapids here of what was indeed a novel craft to these waters. They waved their caps and gave us a cheery shout as we quickly disappeared around another curve; but while it still rung in our ears we were suddenly confronted by one of the tightest fences on the course, and had neither time nor disposition to return the salute.

And so we slid along, down rapids, through long stretches of quiet water and scraping over shallows, plying both oars and paddle, while now and then "making" a fence and comparing its savagery with that of the preceding one. Here and there the high vine-clad banks, from overshadowing us would irregularly recede, leaving little meadows, full of painted-cups, the wild rose-colored phlox and saxifrage; or bits of woodland in the dryer bottoms, radiant, amid the underbrush, with the daisy, cinque-foil, and puccoon. Kingfishers and blue herons abound. Great turtles, disturbed by the unwonted splash of oars, slide down high, sunny banks of sand, where they have been to lay their eggs, and amid a cloud of dust shuffle off into the water, their castle of safety. These eggs, so trustfully left to be hatched by the warmth of the sun, form toothsome food for coons and skunks, which in turn fall victims to farmers' lads, — as witness the rows of peltries stretched inside out on shingles, and tacked up on the sunny sides of the barns and woodsheds along the river highway.

As we begin to approach the valley of the Rock, the hills grow higher, groups of red cedar appear, the banks of red clay often attain the height of fifty or sixty feet, broken by deep, staring gullies and wooded ravines, through which little brooklets run, the output of back-country springs; while the pocket-meadows are less frequent, although more charmingly diversified as to color and background.

We had our mid-day lunch on a pleasant bank, that had been covered earlier in the season with hepatica, blood-root, and dicentra, and was now resplendent with Solomon's seal, the dark-purple water-leaf, and graceful maiden-hair ferns, with here and there a dogwood in full bloom. Behind us were thick woods and an overlooking ridge; opposite, a meadow-glade on which herds of cattle and black hogs grazed. A bell cow waded into the water, followed by several other members of the herd, and the train pensively proceeded in single file diagonally across the shallow stream to another feeding-ground below. The leader's bell had a peculiarly mournful note, and the scene strongly reminded one of an ecclesiastical procession.

In the middle of the afternoon the little village of Fulton was reached. It is a dead-alive, moss-grown settlement, situated on a prairie, through which the river has cut a deep channel. There are a cheese-factory, a grist-mill, a church, a school-house, three or four stores, and some twenty-five houses, with but a solitary boat in sight, and that of the punt variety. It was recess at the school as we rowed past, and boys and girls were chiefly engaged in climbing the trees which cluster in the little schoolhouse yard. A chorus of shouts and whistles greeted us from the leafy perches, in which we could distinguish "Shoot the roof!"— an exclamation called forth by the awning, which doubtless seemed the chief feature of our outfit, viewed from the top of the bank.

At the mill-dam, a dozen lazy, shiftless fellows were fishing at the foot of the chute, and stared at our movements with expressionless eyes. The portage was somewhat difficult, being over a high bank, across a rocky road, and down through a stretch of bog. When we had completed the carry, W—— waited in the canoe while I went up to the fishermen for information as to the lay of the country.

"How far is it to the mouth of the Catfish, my friend?" I asked the most intelligent member of the party.

"D'no! Never was thar." He jerked in his bait, to pull off a weed that had become entangled in it, and from the leer he gave his comrades it was plain that I had struck the would-be wag of the village.

"How far do you think it is?" I insisted, curious to see how far he would carry his obstinacy.

"Don' think nuthin' 'bout 't; don' care t' know."

"Did n't you ever hear any one say how far it is?" and I sat beside him on the stone pier, as if I had come to stay.

"Nah!"

"Suppose you were placed in a boat here and had to float down to the Rock, how long do you imagine you'd be?"

"Aint no man goin' t' place me in no boat! No siree!" pugnaciously.

"Don't you ever row?"

"Nah!" contemptuously; "what I want of a boat? Bridge 's good 'nough fer us fellers, a-fishin'."

"Whose boat is that, over there, on the shore?"

"Schoolmaster's. He's a dood, he is. Bridge is n't rich 'nough fer his blood. Boats is fer doods." And with this withering remark he relapsed into so intent an observation of his line that I thought it best to disturb him no longer.

Below Fulton, the stream is quite swift and the scenery more rugged, the evidences of disastrous spring overflows and back-water from the Rock being visible on every hand. At five o'clock, we came to a point where the river divides into three channels, there being a clump of four small islands. A barbed-wire fence, the last we were fated to meet, was stretched across each channel. Selecting the central mouth,—for this is the delta of the Catfish,—we shot down with a rush, but were soon lodged on a sandbank. It required wading and much pushing and twisting and towing before we were again off, but in the length of a few rods more we swung free into the Rock, which was to be our highway for over two hundred miles more of canoe travel.

The Rock River is nearly a quarter of a mile wide at this point, and comes down with a majestic sweep from the north, having its chief source in the gloomily picturesque Lake Koshkonong. The banks of the river at and below the mouth of the Catfish, are quite imposing, rising into a succession of graceful, round-topped mounds, from fifty to one hundred feet high, and finely wooded except where cleared for pasture or as the site of farm-buildings. While the immediate edges of the stream are generally firm and grass-grown, with occasional gravelly beaches, there are frequent narrow strips of marsh at the bases of the mounds, especially on the left bank where innumerable springs send forth trickling rills to feed the river. A stiff wind up-stream had broken the surface into white caps, and more than counteracted the force of the lazy current, so that progress now depended upon vigorous exercise at the oars and paddle.

Three miles above Janesville is Pope's

Springs, a pleasant summer resort, with white tents and gayly painted cottages commingled. It is situated in a park-like wood, on the right bank, while directly opposite are some bold, rocky cliffs, or palisades, their feet laved in the stream. We spread our supper cloth on the edge of a wheat-field, in view of the pretty scene. The sun was setting behind a bank of roseate clouds, and shooting up broad, sharply defined bands of radiance nearly to the zenith. The wind was blowing cold, wraps were essential, and we were glad to be on our way once more, paddling along in the dying light, past palisades and fields and meadows, reaching prosperous Janesville, on her rolling prairie, just as dusk was thickening into dark.

CHAPTER III.

AN ILLINOIS PRAIRIE HOME.

WE had an early start from the hotel next morning. A prospect of the situation at the upper Janesville dam, from a neighboring bridge, revealed the fact that the mill-race along the left bank afforded the easiest portage. Reloading our craft at the boat-renter's staging where it had passed the night, we darted across the river, under two low-hung bridges, keeping well out of the overflow current and entered the race, making our carry over a steep and rocky embankment.

Below, after passing through the centre of the city, the river widens considerably, as it cuts a deep channel through the fertile prairie, and taking a sudden bend to the southwest, becomes a lake, formed by back-water from the lower dam. The wind was now dead ahead again, and fierce. White caps came savagely rolling up stream. The pull down brought out the rowing muscles to their fullest tension. The canoe at times would appear to scarcely creep along, although oars and paddle would bend to their work.

The race of the carding-mill, which we were now approaching, is by the left bank, the rest of the broad river — fully a third of a mile wide here — being stemmed by a ponderous, angling dam, the shorter leg of which comes dangerously close to the entrance of the race, which it nearly parallels. Overhead, fifty feet skyward, a great railway bridge spans the chasm. The disposition of its piers leaves a rowing channel but two rods wide, next the shore. Through this a deep, swift current flows, impelling itself for the most part over the short leg of the chute, with a deafening roar. Its backset, however, is caught in the yawning mouth of the race. It so happens then that from either side of an ugly whirling strip of doubting water, parallel with the shorter chute, the flood bursts forth, — to the left plunging impetuously over the apron to be dashed to vapor at its foot; to the right madly rushing into the narrow race, to turn the wheels of the carding-mill half a mile below. This narrow channel, under the bridge and next the shore, of which I have spoken, is the only practicable entrance to the race.

We had landed above and taken a panoramic view of the situation from the deck of the bridge; afterward had descended to the flood-gates at the entrance of the race, for detailed inspection and measurements. One of the set of three gates was partly raised, the bottom being but three feet above the boiling surface, while the great vertical iron beams along which the cog-wheels work were not over four feet apart. It would require steady hands to guide the canoe to the right of the whirl, where the flood hesitated between two destinations, and finally to shoot under the uplifted gate, which barely gave room in either height or breadth for the passage of the boat. But we arrived at the conclusion that the shoot was far more dangerous in appearance than in reality, and that it was preferable to a long and exceedingly irksome portage.

So we determined to make the attempt, and walked back to the canoe. Disposing our baggage in the centre, as in the barbed-wire experience of the day before, W—— again took the oars astern and I the paddle at the bow. A knot of men on the bridge had been watching our movements with interest, and waved their hats at us as we came cautiously creeping along the shore. We went under the bridge with a swoop, waited till we were within three rods of the brink of the thundering fall, and then strained every muscle in sending the canoe shooting off at an angle into the waters bound for the race. We went down to the gate as if shot out of a cannon, but the little craft was easily controlled, quickly obeying every stroke of the paddle. Catching a projecting timber, it was easy to guide ourselves to the opening. We lay down in the bottom of the boat and with uplifted hands clutched the slimy gate; slowly, hand over hand, we passed through under the many internal beams and rods of the structure, with the boiling flood under us, making an echoing roar, amid which we were obliged to fairly shout our directions to each other. In the last section the release was given; we were fairly hurled into daylight on the surface of the mad torrent, and were many a rod down the race before we could recover our seats. The men on the bridge, joined by others, now fairly yelled themselves hoarse over the successful close of what was apparently a hazardous venture, and we waved acknowledgments with the paddle, as we glided away under the willows which overhang the long and narrow canal. At the isolated mill, where there is one of the easiest portages on the route, the hands came flocking by dozens to the windows to see the craft which had invaded their quiet domain.

The country toward Beloit becomes more hilly, especially upon the left bank, along which runs the Chicago and Northwestern railway, all the way down from Janesville. At the Beloit paper-mill, which was reached at three o'clock in the afternoon, it was found that owing to the low stage of water one end of the apron projected above the flood. With some difficulty as to walking on the slimy incline, we portaged over the face of the dam and went down stream through the heart of the pretty little college town, getting more or less picturesque back-door views of the domestic life of the community.

Beloit being on the State line, we had now entered Illinois. For several miles the river is placid and shallow, with but a feeble current. Islands begin to appear, dividing the channel and somewhat perplexing canoeists, it being often quite difficult to decide which route is the best; as a rule, one is apt to wish that he had taken some other than the one selected.

The dam at Rockton was reached in a two hours' pull. It was being repaired, stone for the purpose being quarried on a neighboring bank and transported to the scene of action on a flat-boat. We had been told that we could save several miles by going down the race, which cuts the base of a long detour. But the boss of the dam-menders assured us that the race was not safe, and that we would "get in a trap" if we attempted it. Deeming discretion the better part of valor, with much difficulty we lifted the canoe over the high, jagged, stone embankment and through a bit of tangled swamp to the right, and took the longest way around. It was four or five miles by the bend to the village of Rockton, whose spires we could see at the dam, rising above a belt of intervening trees. It being our first detour of note, we were somewhat discouraged at having had so long a pull for so short a vantage; but we became well used to such experiences long before our journey was over. It was not altogether consoling to be informed at Rockton — which is a smart little manufacturing town of a thousand souls — that the race was perfectly practicable for canoes, and the tail portage easy.

Beaching near the base of a fine wagon-bridge which here spans the Rock, we went up to a cluster of small houses on the bank opposite the town, to have some tea steeped, our prepared stock being by this time exhausted. The people were all employed in the paper-mills in the village, but one good woman chanced to be at home for the afternoon, and cheerfully responded to our request for service. A young, neat, and buxom little woman she was, though rather sad-eyed and evidently overworked in the family struggle for existence. She assured us that she nowadays never went upon the water in an open boat, for she had "three times been near drowndid" in her life, which she thought was "warnin' enough for one body." Inquiry developed that her first "warnin'" consisted of having been, when she was "a gal down in Kansis," taken for a row in a leaky boat; the water came in half-way up to the thwarts, and would have eventually swamped the craft and drowned its occupants, in perhaps half an hour's time, if her companion had not luckily bethought himself to run in to shore and land. Another time, she and her husband were out rowing, when a stern-wheel river steamer came along, and the swell in her wake washed the row-boat atop of a log raft, and "she stuck there, ma'am, would ye believe, and we'd 'a' drowndid sure, with a storm a-comin' up, had n't my brother-in-law, that was then a-courtin' of sister Jane, come off in a dug-out and took us in." Her last and most harrowing experience was in a boat on the Republican River in Kansas. She and another woman were out when a storm came up, and white-capped waves tossed the little craft about at will ; but fortunately the blow subsided, and the women regained pluck enough to take the oars and row home again. The eyes of the paper-maker's wife were suffused with tears, as, seated in her rocking-chair by the kitchen stove and giving the tea-pot an occasional shake, doubtless to hasten the brew, she related these thrilling tales of adventure by flood, and called us to witness that thrice had Providence directly interposed in her behalf. We were obliged to acknowledge ourselves much impressed with the gravity of the dangers she had so successfully passed through. Her sympathy with the perils which we were braving, in what she was pleased to call our singular journey, was so great that the good woman declined to accept pay for having steeped our tea in a most excellent manner, and bade us an affecting God-speed.

We had our supper, graced with the hot tea, on a pretty sward at the river end of the quiet lane just around the corner; while a dozen little children in pinafores and short clothes, perched on a neighboring fence, watched and discussed us as eagerly as though we were a circus caravan halting by the wayside for refreshment. The paper-maker's wife also came out, just as we were packing up for the start, and inspected the canoe in some detail. Her judgment was that in her giddiest days as an oarswoman, she would certainly never have dared to set foot in such a shell. She watched us off, just as the sun was disappearing, and the last Rockton object we saw was our tender-hearted friend standing on the beach at the end of her lane, both hands shading her eyes, as she watched us fade away in the gloaming. I have no doubt she has long ago given us up for lost, for her last words were, "I've heerd 'em tell it was a riskier river than any in Kansis, 'tween here an' Missip'; tek care ye don't git drowndid!"

In the soft evening shadows it was cool enough for heavy wraps. In fact, for the greater part of the day W—— had worn a light shoulder cape. We had a beautiful sunset, back of a group of densely timbered islands. We would have been sorely tempted to camp out on one of these, but the night was setting in too cold for sleeping in the open air, and we had no tent with us.

The twilight was nearly spent, and the

banks and now frequent islands were so heavily wooded that on the river it was rapidly becoming too dark to navigate among the shallows and devious channels. W—— volunteered to get out and look for a farmhouse, for none could be seen from our hollow way. So she landed and got up into some prairie wheatfields back away from the bank. After a half-mile's walk parallel with the river she sighted a prosperous-looking establishment, with a smart windmill, large barns, and a thrifty orchard, silhouetted against the fast-fading sunset sky. The signal was given, and the prow of the canoe was soon resting on a steep, gravely beach at the mouth of a ravine. Armed with the paddle, for a possible encounter with dogs, we went up through the orchard and a timothy-field sopping with dew, scaled the barnyard fence, passed a big black dog that growled savagely, but was by good chance chained to an old mowing-machine, walked up to the kitchen door and boldly knocked.

No answer. The stars were coming out, the shadows darkening, night was fairly upon us, and shelter must be had, if we were obliged to sleep in the barn. The dog reared on his hind legs, and fairly howled with rage. A row of well-polished milk-cans on a bench by the windmill well, and the general air of thrifty neatness impelled us to persevere. An old German, with kindly face and bushy white hair, finally came, cautiously peering out beneath a candle which he held above his head. English he had none, and our German was too fresh from the books to be reliable in conversation. However, we mustered a few stereotyped phrases from the "familiar conversations" in the back of the grammar, which served to make the old man smile, and disappearing toward the cattle-sheds he soon returned with his daughter and son-in-law, a cheerful young couple who spoke good English, and assured us of welcome and a bed. They had been out milking by lantern-light when interrupted, and soon rejoined us with brimming pails.

It did not take long to feel quite at home with these simple, good-hearted folk. They had but recently purchased the farm and were strangers in the community. The old man lived with his other children at Freeport, and was there only upon a visit. The young people, natives of Illinois, were lately married, their wedding-trip having been made to this house, where they had at once settled down to a thrifty career, surrounded with quite enough comforts for all reasonable demands, and a few simple luxuries. W—— declared the kitchen to be a model of neatness and convenience; and the sitting-room, where we passed the evening with our modest entertainers, — who appeared quite well posted on current news of general importance, — showed evidences of being in daily use. They were devout Catholics, and I was pleased to find the patriarch drifting down the river of time with a heartfelt appreciation of the benefits of democracy, fully cognizant of what American institutions had done for him and his. Immigrating in the noon-tide of life and settling in a German neighborhood, he had found no need and had no inclination to learn our language. But he had prospered from the start, had secured for his children a good education at the common schools, had imbued them with the spirit of patriotism, had seen them marry happily and with a bright future, and at night he never retired without uttering a bedside prayer of gratitude that God had turned his footsteps to blessed America. As the old man told me his tale, with his daughter's hands resting lovingly in his while she served as our interpreter, and contrasted the hard lot of a German peasant with the independence of thought and speech and action vouchsafed the German-American farmer, who can win competence in a state of freedom, I felt a thrill of patriotism that would have been the making of a Fourth-of-July orator. I wished that thousands such as he originally was, still dragging out an existence in the fatherland, could have listened to my aged friend and followed in his footsteps.

CHAPTER IV.

THE HALF-WAY HOUSE.

THE spin down to Roscoe next morning was delightful in every respect. The air was just sharp enough for vigorous exercise. These were the pleasantest hours we had yet spent. The blisters that had troubled us for the first three days were hardening into callosities, and arm and back muscles, which at first were sore from the unusually heavy strain upon them, at last were strengthened to their work. Thereafter we felt no physical inconvenience from our self-imposed task. At night, after a pull of eleven or twelve hours, relieved only by the time spent in lunching, in which we hourly alternated at the oars and paddle, slumber came as a most welcome visitation, while the morning ever found us as fresh as at the start. Let those afflicted with insomnia try this sort of life. My word for it, they will not be troubled so long as the canoeing continues. Every muscle of the body moves responsive to each pull of the oars or sweep of the paddle; while the mental faculties are kept continually on the alert, watching for shallows, snags, and rapids, in which operation a few days' experience will render one quite expert, though none the less cautious.

As we get farther down into the Illinois country, the herds of live-stock increase in size and number. Cattle may be seen by hundreds at one view, dotted all over the neighboring hills and meadows, or dreamily standing in the cooling stream at sultry noonday. Sheep, in immense flocks, bleat in deafening unison, the ewes and their young being particularly demonstrative at our appearance, and sometimes excitedly following us along the banks. Droves of black hogs and shoats are ploughing the sward in their search for sweet roots, or lying half-buried in the wet sand. Horses, in familiar groups, quickly lift their heads in startled wonder as the canopied canoe glides silently by, — then suddenly wheel, kick up their heels, sound a snort of alarm, and dash off at a thundering gallop, clods of turf filling the air behind them. There are charming groves and parks and treeless downs, and the river cuts through the alluvial soil to a depth of eight and ten feet, throwing up broad beaches on either side.

At Roscoe, three or four miles below our morning's starting-point, there is a collection of three or four neat farm-houses, each with its spinning windmill.

Latham Station, nine miles below Rockton, was reached at ten o'clock. The post-office is called Owen. There is a smart little depot on the Chicago, Milwaukee, and St. Paul railway line, two general stores, and a half-dozen cottages, with a substantial-looking creamery, where we obtained buttermilk drawn fresh from one of the mammoth churns. The concern manufactures from three hundred to nine hundred pounds per day, according to the season, shipping chiefly to New York city. Leaning over the hand-rail which fences off the "making" room, and gossiping with the young man in charge, I conjured up visions of the days when, as a boy on the farm, I used to spend many weary, almost tearful hours, pounding an old crock churn, in which the butter would always act like a balky horse and refuse to "come" until after a long series of experimental coaxing. Nowadays, rustic youths luxuriously ride behind the plough, the harrow, the cultivator, the horse-rake, the hay-loader, and the self-binding harvester, while

The Half-Way House.   77

the butter-making is farmed out to a factory where the thing is done by steam. The farmer's boy of the future will live in a world darkened only by the frown of the district schoolmaster and the intermittent round of stable chores.

At Latham Station we encountered the first ferry-boat on our trip, — a flat-bottomed scow with side-rails, attached by ropes and

> FARE.
>
> Foot Passengere . .   10 cts.
> Man & Horse . . .   15 ct.
> single Carriage . . .   10 c.
> double   "   . . .   15 c
> each Passinger . . . .5 c
>
> Night Raites . . Double Fare.
>
> All persons
> Are cautioned
> Againts useing
> this Boat with Out
> Permistion from
> the Owners

pulleys to a suspended wire cable, and working diagonally, with the force of the current. A sign conspicuously displayed on the craft bore the above legend.

From the time we had entered Illinois, the large, graceful, white blossoms of the Pennsylvanian anemone and the pink and white fringe of the erigeron Canadense had appeared in great abundance upon the river banks, while the wild prairie rose lent a delicate beauty and fragrance to the scene. On sandy knolls, where in early spring the anemone patens and crowfoot violets had thrived in profusion, were now to be seen the geum triflorum and the showy yellow puccoon; the long-flowered puccoon, with its delicate pale yellow, crape-like blossom, was just putting in an appearance; and little white, star-shaped flowers, which were strangers to us of Wisconsin, fairly dotted the green hillsides, mingled in striking contrast with dwarf blue mint. Bevies of great black crows, sitting in the tops of dead willow-trees or circling around them, rent the air with sepulchral squawks. Men and boys were cultivating in the cornfields, the prevalent drought painfully evidenced by the clouds of gray dust which enveloped them and their teams as they stirred up the brittle earth.

There was now a fine breeze astern, and the awning, abandoned during the head winds of the day before, was again welcomed as the sun mounted to the zenith. At 2.30 P. M.,

The Half-Way House.   79

we were in busy Rockford, where the banks are twenty or twenty-five feet high, with rolling prairies stretching backward to the horizon, except where here and there a wooded ridge intervenes. Rockford is the metropolis of the valley of the Rock. It has twenty-two thousand inhabitants, with many elegant mansions visible from the river, and evidences upon every hand of that prosperity which usually follows in the train of varied manufacturing enterprises.

There are numerous mills and factories along both sides of the river, and a protracted inspection of the portage facilities was necessary before we could **decide** on which bank to make our carry. The right was chosen. The portage was somewhat over two ordinary city blocks in length, up a steep incline and through a road-way tunnel under a great flouring mill. We had made **nearly** half the distance, and were resting for a moment, when a mill-driver kindly offered the use of his wagon, which was gratefully accepted. We were soon spinning down the tail of the race, a half-dozen millers waving **a** "Chautauqua salute" with as many dusty flour-bags, and in ten minutes more had left Rockford out of sight.

Several miles below, th**ere** are a half-dozen

forested islands in a bunch, some of them four or five acres in extent, and we puzzled over which channel to take,—the best of them abounding in shallows. The one down which the current seemed to set the strongest was selected, but we had not proceeded over half a mile before the trees on the banks began to meet in arches overhead, and it was evident that we were ascending a tributary. It proved to be the Cherry River, emptying into the main stream from the east. The wind, now almost due-west, had driven the waves into the mouth of the Cherry, so that we mistook this surface movement for the current. Coming to a railway bridge, which we knew from our map did not cross the Rock, our course was retraced, and after some difficulty with snags and gravel-spits, we were once more upon our proper highway, trending to the southwest.

Supper was eaten upon the edge of a large island, several miles farther down stream, in the shade of two wide-spreading locusts. Opposite are some fine, eroded sandstone palisades, which formation had been frequently met with during the day,—sometimes on both sides of the river, but generally on the left bank, which is, as a rule, the most picturesque along the entire course.

It was still so cold when evening shadows thickened that camping out, with our meagre preparations for it, seemed impracticable; so we pushed on and kept a sharp lookout for some friendly farm-house at which to quarter for the night. The houses in the thickly-wooded bottoms, however, were generally quite forbidding in appearance, and the sun had gone down before we sighted a well-built stone dwelling amid a clump of graceful evergreens. It seemed, from the river, to be the very embodiment of comfortable neatness; but upon ascending the gentle slope and fighting off two or three mangy curs which came snarling at our heels, we found the structure merely a relic of gentility. There was scarcely a whole pane of glass in the house, there were eight or ten wretchedly dirty and ragged children, the parents were repulsive in appearance and manner, and a glimpse of the interior presented a picture of squalor which would have shocked a city missionary. The stately stone house was a den of the most abject and shiftless poverty, the like of which one could seldom see in the slums of a metropolis. These people were in the midst of a splendid farming country, had an abundance of pure air and water at command, and there seemed to be no excuse for their condition. Drink and laziness were doubtless the besetting sins in this uncanny home. Making a pretense of inquiring the distance to Byron, the next village below, we hurried from the accursed spot.

A half-hour later we reached the high bridge of the Chicago, Milwaukee and St. Paul railway, above Byron, and ran our bow on a little beach at the base of the left bank, which is here thirty feet high. A section-man had a little cabin hard by, and his gaunt, talkative wife, with a chubby little boy by her side, had been keenly watching our approach from her garden-fence. She greeted us with a shrill but cheery voice as we clambered up a zigzag path and joined her upon the edge of the prairie.

"Good ev'nin', folks! Whar 'n earth d' ye come from?"

We enlightened her in a few words.

"Don't mean t' say ye come all the way from Weesconsin a' down here in that thing?" pointing down at the canoe, which certainly looked quite small, at that depth, in the dim twilight.

"Certainly; why not?"

"Ye'll git drowndid, an' I'm not mistakin, afore ye git to Byron."

"River dangerous, ma'am?"

"Dang'rous ain't no name for 't. There was a young feller drowndid at this here bridge las' spring. The young feller he worked at the bridge-mendin', bein' a carpenter,—he called himself a carpenter, but he war n't no great fist at carpenterin', an' I know it,—and he boarded up at Byron. A 'nsurance agint kim 'long and got Rollins,— the young feller his name was Abe Rollins, an' he was a bach,— to promise to 'sure his life for a thousand dollars, which was to go t' his sister, what takes in washin', an' her man ran away from her las' year an' nobody knows where he is,— which I says is good riddance, but she takes on as though she had los' somebody worth cryin' over: there's no accountin' for tastes. The agint says to Rollins to go over to the doctor's of'c' to git 'xamined and Rollins says, 'No, I ain't agoin' to git 'xamined till I clean off; I'll go down an' take a swim at the bridge and then come back and strip for the doctor.' An' Rollins he took his swim and got sucked down inter a hole just yonder down there, by the openin' of Stillman's Creek, and he was a corpse when they hauled him out, down off Byron; an' he never hollered once but jist sunk like a stone with a cramp; an' his folks never got no 'nsurance money at all, for lackin' the doctor's c'tificate. An' it's heaps o' folks git drowndid in this river, an' nobody ever hears of 'em agin; an' I would n't no more step foot in that boat nor the biggest ship on the sea, an' I don't see how you can do it, ma'am!"

No doubt the good woman would have rattled on after this fashion for half the night, but we felt obliged, owing to the rapidly increasing darkness, to interrupt her with geographical inquiries. She assured us that Byron was distant some five or six miles by river, with, so far as she had heard, many shallows, whirlpools, and snags *en route;* while by land the village was but a mile and a quarter across the prairie, from the bridge. We accordingly made fast for the night where we had landed, placed our heaviest baggage in the tidy kitchen-sitting-room-parlor of our voluble friend, and trudged off over the fields to Byron, — a solitary light in a window and the occasional practice-note of a brass band, borne to us on the light western breeze, being our only guides.

After a deal of stumbling over a rough and ill-defined path, which we could distinguish by the sense of feeling alone, we finally reached the exceedingly quiet little village, and by dint of inquiry from house to house, — in most of which the denizens seemed preparing to retire for the night, — found the inn which had been recommended by the sectionman's wife as the best in town. It was the only one. There were several commercial travelers in the place, and the hostelry was filled. But the landlord kindly surrendered to us his own well-appointed chamber, above an empty store where the village band was tuning up for Decoration Day. It seemed appropriate enough that there should be music to greet us, for we were now one hundred and thirty-four miles from Madison, and practically half through our voyage to the Mississippi.

CHAPTER V.

GRAND DETOUR FOLKS.

WE tramped back to the bridge in high spirits next morning, over the flower-strewn prairie. The section-man's wife was on hand, with her entire step-laddered brood of six, to see us off. As we carried down our traps to the beach and repacked, she kept up a continuous strain of talk, giving us a most edifying review of her life, and especially the particulars of how she and her "man" had first romantically met, while he was a gravel-train hand on a far western railroad, and she the cook in a portable construction-barracks.

Stillman's Creek opens into the Rock from the east, through a pleasant glade, a few rods below the bridge. We took a pull up this historic tributary for a half-mile or more. It is a muddy stream, some two and a half rods wide, cutting down for a half-dozen feet through the black soil. The shores are generally well fringed with heavy timber, especially upon the northern bank, while the land to the south and southwest stretches upward, in gentle slopes, to a picturesque rolling prairie, abounding in wooded knolls. It was in the large grove on the north bank, near its junction with the Rock, that Black Hawk, in the month of May, 1832, parleyed with the Pottawattomies. It was here that on the 14th of that month he learned of the treachery of Stillman's militiamen, and at once made that famous sally with his little band of forty braves which resulted in the rout of the cowardly whites, who fled pell-mell over the prairie toward Dixon, asserting that Black Hawk and two thousand blood-thirsty warriors were sweeping northern Illinois with the besom of destruction. The country round about appears to have undergone no appreciable change in the half-century intervening between that event and to-day. The topographical descriptions given in contemporaneous accounts of Stillman's flight will hold good now, and we were readily able to pick out the points of interest on the old battlefield.

Returning to the Rock, we made excellent progress. The atmosphere was bracing; and there being a favoring northwest breeze, our awning was stretched over a hoop for a sail. The banks were now steep inclines of white sand and gravel. It was like going through a railroad cut. But in ascending the sides, as we did occasionally, to secure supplies from farm-houses or refill our canteen with fresh water, there were found broad expanses of rolling prairie. The farm establishments increase in number and prosperity. Windmills may be counted by the scores, the cultivation of enormous cornfields is everywhere in progress, and cattle are more numerous than ever.

Three or four miles above Oregon the banks rise to the dignity of hills, which come sweeping down "with verdure clad" to the very water's edge, and present an inspiring picture, quite resembling some of the most charming stretches of the Hudson. At the entrance to this lovely vista we encountered a logy little pleasure-steamer anchored in the midst of the stream, which is here nearly half of a mile wide, for the river now perceptibly broadens. The captain, a ponderous old sea-dog, wearing a cowboy's hat and having the face of an operatic pirate, with a huge pipe between his black teeth, sat lounging on the bulwark, watching the force of the current, into which he would listlessly expectorate. He was at first inclined to be surly, as we hauled alongside and checked our course; but gradually softened down as we drew him out in conversation, and confided to us that he had in earlier days "sailed the salt water," a circumstance of which he seemed very proud. He also gave us some "pointers on the lay o' the land," as he called them, for our future guidance down the river, — one of which was that there were "dandy sceneries" below Oregon, in comparison with which we had thus far seen nothing worthy of note. As for himself, he said that his place on the neighboring shore was connected by telephone with Oregon, and his steamer frequently transported pleasure parties to points of interest above the dam.

Ganymede Spring is on the southeast bank, at the base of a lofty sandstone bluff, a mile or so above Oregon. From the top of the bluff, which is ascended by a succession of steep flights of scaffolding stairs, a magnificent bird's-eye view is attainable of one of the finest river and forest landscapes in the Mississippi basin. The grounds along the riverside at the base are laid out in graceful carriage drives; and over the head of a neatly hewn basin, into which gushes the copious spring, is a marble slab thus inscribed: —

> GANYMEDE'S SPRINGS,
> named by
> MARGERET FULLER (Countess D. Ossoli,)
> who named this bluff
> EAGLE'S NEST,
> & beneath the cedars on its crest wrote
> "Ganymede to his Eagle,"
> July 4, 1843.

Oregon was reached just before noon. A walk through the business quarter revealed a thrifty, but oldish-looking town of about two thousand inhabitants. The portage on the east side, around a flouring-mill dam, involved a hard pull up the gravelly bank thirty feet high, and a haul of two blocks' length along a dusty street.

There was a fine stretch of eroded palisades in front of the island on which we lunched. The color effect was admirable, — patches of gray, brown, white, and old gold, much corroded with iron. Vines of many varieties dangle from earth-filled crevices, and swallows by the hundreds occupy the dimples neatly hollowed by the action of the water in some ancient period when the stream was far broader and deeper than now.

But at times, even in our day, the Rock is

a raging torrent. The condition of the trees along the river banks and on the thickly-strewn island pastures, shows that not many months before it must have been on a wild rampage, for the great trunks are barked by the ice to the height of fifteen feet above the present water-level. Everywhere, on banks and islands, are the evidences of disastrous floods, and the ponderous ice-breakers above the bridges give one an awesome notion of the condition of affairs at such a time. Farmers assured us that in the spring of 1887 the water was at the highest stage ever recorded in the history of the valley. Many of the railway bridges barely escaped destruction, while the numerous river ferries and the low country bridges in the bayous were destroyed by scores. The banks were overflowed for miles together, and back in the country for long distances, causing the hasty removal of families and live-stock from the bottoms; while ice jams, forming at the heads of the islands, would break, and the shattered floes go sweeping down with terrific force, crushing the largest trees like reeds, tearing away fences and buildings, covering islands and meadows with deep deposits of sand and mud, blazing their way through the forested banks, and creating sad havoc on every hand.

We were amply convinced, by the thousands of broken trees which littered our route, the snags, the mud-baked islands, the frequent stretches of sadly demoralized bank that had not yet had time to reweave its charitable mantle of verdure, that the Rock, on such a spring "tear," must indeed be a picture of chaos broken loose. This explained why these hundreds of beautiful and spacious islands — many of them with charming combinations of forest and hillock and meadow, and occasionally enclosing pretty ponds blushing with water-lilies — are none of them inhabited, but devoted to the pasture of cattle, who swim or ford the intervening channels, according to the stage of the flood; also why the picturesque bottoms on the main shore are chiefly occupied by the poorest class of farmers, who eke out their meagre incomes with the spoils of the gun and line.

It was a quarter of five when we beached at the upper ferry-landing at Grand Detour. It is a little, tumble-down village of one or two small country stores, a church, and a dozen modest cottages; there is also, on the river front, a short row of deserted shops, their paintless battlement-fronts in a sadly collapsed condition, while hard by are the ruins of two or three dismantled mills. The settlement is on a **bit of prairie at the base of** the preliminary flourish of the "big bend" of **the Rock,—hence the name, Grand** Detour, a reminiscence of **the early** French explorers. The foot of the peninsula is but half a mile across, while the distance around by **river to** the lower ferry, on the other side of the village is four miles. Having learned that the bottoms below here were, for a long distance, peculiarly gloomy and but sparsely inhabited, we thought it best to pass the night at Grand Detour. Bespeaking accommodations at the tavern and post-office combined, we rowed **around** the bend to the lower landing, through **some** lovely **stretches of river scenery,** in which **bold** palisades and delightful little meadows predominated.

The walk back to the village was through a fine park of elms. The stage was just in from Dixon, with the mail. There was an eager little knot of villagers in the cheerful sitting-room of our homelike inn, watching the stout landlady as she distributed it in a checker-board rank of glass-faced boxes fenced off in front of a sunny window. It **did** not appear that many of those who over**looked the** distribution of the mail had been favored by their correspondents. They were chiefly concerned in seeing who did get letters and papers, and in "passin' the time o' day," as gossiping is called in rural communities. Seated in a darkened corner, waiting patiently for supper, the announcement of which was an hour or more in coming, we were much amused at the mirror of local events which was unconsciously held up for us by these loungers of both sexes and all ages, who fairly filled the room, and oftentimes waxed hot in controversy.

The central theme of conversation was the preparations under way for Decoration Day, which was soon to arrive. Grand Detour was to be favored with a speaker from Dixon, — " a reg'lar major from the war, gents, an' none o' yer m'lish fellers!" an enthusiastic old man with a crutch persisted in announcing. There were to be services at the church, and some exercises at the cemetery, where lie buried the half-dozen honored dead, Grand Detour's sacrifice upon the altar of the Union. The burning question seemed to be whether the village preacher would consent to offer prayer upon the occasion, if the church choir insisted on being accompanied on the brand-new cabinet organ which the congregation had voted to purchase, but to which the pastor and one of the leading deacons were said to be bitterly opposed, as smacking of worldliness and **antichrist**. Only the evening before, this deacon, armed with a sledge-hammer and rope, had been seen to go to the sanctuary in **company** with his "hired man," and enter through one of the windows, which they pried up for the purpose. A good gossip, who lived hard by, closely watched such extraordinary proceedings. There was a great noise within, then some planks were pitched out of the window, soon followed by the deacon and his man. The window was shut down, the planks thrown atop of the horse-shed roof, and the **men** disappeared. Investigation in the morning by the witness revealed the fact that the choir-seats and **the** organ-platform had been torn down and removed. Here was a pretty **how d' do!** The wiry, raspy little woman, with her gray finger-curls and withered, simpering smile, had, with **great** forbearance, kept her choice bit of news to herself till " post-office time." Sitting in **a big** rocking-chair close to the delivery window, knitting vigorously on an elongated stocking, **she** demurely asserted that she "never wanted to say **nothin'** 'gin' nobody, or to hurt nobody's feelin's," and then detailed the entire circumstance to the patrons **of** the office as they came **in**. The excitement created by the story, which doubtless lost nothing in the telling, was at fever-heat. We were sorely tempted to remain over till Decoration Day, — when, it was freely predicted, there " would be some folks as 'd wish they 'd never been born," — and see the outcome of this tempest in a teapot. But our programme, unfortunately, would not admit of such a diversion.

Others came and went, but the gossipy little body with the gray curls rocked on, holding converse with both post-mistress and public, keeping a keen eye on the character of the mail matter obtained by the villagers and neighboring farmers, and freely commenting on it all; so that new-comers were kept quite well-informed as to the correspondence of those who had just departed.

A sad-eyed little woman in rusty black modestly slipped in, and was handed out a much-creased and begrimed envelope, which she nervously clutched. She was hurrying silently away, when the gossip sharply exclaimed, " Good lands, Cynthi' Prescott! some folks don't know a body when they meet. 'Spose ye 've been hearin' from Jim at last. I 'd been thinkin' 't was about time ye got a letter from his hand, ef he war ever goin' t' write at all. Tell ye, Cynthi' Prescott,

ye 're too indulgent on that man o' yourn!
Ef I — "

But Cynthia Prescott, turning her black, deep-sunken eyes to her inquisitor, with a piteous, tearful look, as though stung to the quick, sidled out backward through the wire-screen door, which sprung closed with a vicious bang, and I saw her hurrying down the village street firmly grasping at her bosom what the mail had brought her, — probably a brutal demand for more money, from a worthless husband, who was wrecking his life-craft on some far-away shore.

"Goodness me! but the Gilberts is a-puttin' on style!" ejaculated the village censor, as a rather smart young horseman went out with a bunch of letters, and a little packet tied up in red twine. "That there was vis'tin' keerds from the printer's shop in Dixon, an' cost a dollar; can't fool me! There's some folks as hev to be leavin' keerds on folks's centre-tables when they goes makin' calls, for fear folks will be a-forgettin' their names. When I go a-callin', I go a-visitin' and take my work along an' stop an' hev a social cup o' tea; an' they ain't a-goin' to forgit for awhile, that I dropped in on 'em, neither. This way they hev down in Dixon, what I hear of, of ringin' at a bell and settin' down with yer bonnet on and sayin', 'How d' do,' an' a 'Pretty well, I thank yer,' and jumpin' up as if the fire bell was ringin' and goin' on through the whole n'ighberhood as ef ye 're on springs, an' then a-trancin' back home and braggin' how many calls ye 've made, — I ain't got no use for that; it 'll do for Dixon folks, what catch the style from Chicargy, an' they git 't from Paris each year, I 'm told, but I ain't no use for 't. Mebbe ol' man Gilbert is made o' money, — his women folks act so, with all this a-apein' the Clays, who 's been gettin' visitin' keerds all the way from Chicargy, which they ordered of a book agint last fall, with gilt letters an' roses an' sich like in the corners. An' 't was Clay's brother-in-law as tol' me he never did see such carryin's-on over at the old house, with letter-writin' paper sopped in cologne, an' lace curtains in the bed-room winders. An' ye can't tell me but the Gilberts, too, is a-goin' to the dogs, with their paper patterns from Dixon, and dress samples from a big shop in Chicargy, which I seen from the picture on the envelope was as big as all Grand Detour, an' both ferry-landin's thrown in. Grand Detour fashi'ns ain't good 'nough for some folks, I reckon."

And thus the busy-tongued woman discoursed in a vinegary tone upon the characteristics of Grand Detour folks, as illustrated by the nature of the evening mail, frequently interspersing her remarks with a hearty disclaimer of anything malicious in her temperament. At last, however, the supper-bell rang; the doughty postmistress, who had been remarkably discreet throughout all this village tirade, having darted in and out between the kitchen and the office, attending to her dual duties, locked the postal gate with a snap, and asked her now solitary patron, "Anything I can do for you, Maria?" The gossip gathered up her knitting, hastily averred that she had merely dropped in for her weekly paper, but now remembered that this was not the day for it, and ambled off, to reload with venom for the next day's mail.

After supper we walked about the peaceful, pretty, grass-grown village. Shearing was in progress at the barn of the inn, and the streets were filled with bleating sheep and nodding billy-goats. The place presented many evidences of former prosperity, and we were told that a dozen years before it had boasted of a plough factory, two or three flouring-mills, and a good water-power. But the railroad that it was expected would come to Grand Detour had touched Dixon instead, with the result that the village industries had been removed to Dixon, the dam had fallen in, and now there were less than three hundred inhabitants between the two ferries.

When one of the store-keepers told me he had practically no country trade, but that his customers were the villagers alone, I was led to inquire what supported these three hundred people, who had no industries among them, no river traffic, owing to customary low water in summer, and who seemed to live on each other. Many of the villagers, I found, are laborers who work upon the neighboring farms and maintain their families here; a few are farmers, the corners of whose places run down to the village; others there are who either own or rent or "share" farms in the vicinity, going out to their work each day, much of their live stock and crops being housed at their village homes; there are half a dozen retired farmers, who have either sold out their places or have tenants upon them, and live in the village for sociability's sake, or to allow their children the benefit of the excellent local school. Mingled with these people are a shoemaker, a tailor, a storekeeper, who live upon the necessities of their neighbors. Two fishermen spend the summer here, in a tent, selling their daily catch to the villagers and neighboring farmers and occasionally shipping by the daily mail-stage to Dixon, fourteen miles away. The preacher and his family are modestly supported; a young physician wins a scanty subsistence; and for considerably over half the year the schoolmaster shares with them what honors and sorrows attach to these positions of rural eminence. Our pleasant-spoken host was the driver of the Dixon stage, as well as star-route mail contractor, adding the conduct of a farm to his other duties. With his wife as post-mistress, and a pretty, buxom daughter, who waited on our table and was worth her weight in gold, Grand Detour folks said that he was bound to be a millionnaire yet.

As Grand Detour lives, so live thousands of just such little rural villages all over the country. Viewed from the railway track or river channel, they appear to have been once larger than they are to-day. The sight of the unpainted houses, the ruined factory, the empty stores, the grass and weeds in the street, the lack-lustre eyes of the idlers, may induce one to imagine that here is the home of hopeless poverty and despair. But although the railroad which they expected never came; or the railroad which did come went on and scheduled the place as a flag station; still, there is a certain inherent vitality here, an undefined something that holds these people together, a certain degree of hopefulness which cannot rise to the point of ambition, a serene satisfaction with the things that are. Grand Detour folks, and folks like them, are as blissfully content as the denizens of Chicago.

CHAPTER VI.

AN ANCIENT MARINER.

THE clock in a neighboring kitchen was striking six, as we reached the lower ferry-landing. The grass in the streets and under the old elms was as wet with dew as though there had been a heavy shower during the night. The village fishermen were just pulling in to the little pier, returning from an early morning trip to their "traut-lines" down stream. In a long wooden cage, which they towed astern, was a fifty-pound sturgeon, together with several large cat-fish. They kindly hauled their cage ashore, to show us the monsters, which they said would probably be shipped, alive, to a Chicago restaurant which they occasionally furnished with curiosities in their line. These fishermen were rough-looking fellows in their battered hats and ragged, dirty overcoats, with faces sadly in need of water and a shave. They had a sad, pinched-up appearance as well, as though the dense fog, which was but just now yielding to the influence of the sun, had penetrated their bones and given them the chills. On engaging them in friendly conversation about their calling, they exhibited good manners and some knowledge of the outer world. Their business, they said, was precarious and, as we could well see, involved much exposure and hardship. Sometimes it meant a start at midnight, often amid rainstorms, fogs, or chilling weather, with a hard pull back again up-stream, — for their lines were all of them below Grand Detour; but to return with an empty boat, sometimes their luck, was harder yet. Knocking about in this way, all of the year around, — for their winters were similarly spent upon the lower waters and bayous of the Mississippi, — neither of them was ever thoroughly well. One was consumptively inclined, he told me, and being an old soldier, was receiving a small pension. A claim agent had him in hand, however, and his thoughts ran largely upon the prospects of an increase by special legislation. He seemed to have but little doubt that he would ultimately succeed. When he came into this looked-for fortune, he said, he would "quit knockin' 'round an' killin' myself fishin'," settle down in **Grand Detour** for the balance of his days, raising his own "garden sass, pigs, and cow;" and some fine day would make a trip in his boat to the "old home in Injianny, whar I was raised an' 'listed in the war." His face fairly gleamed with pleasure as he thus dwelt upon the flowers of fancy which the pension agent had cultivated within him; and W—— sympathetically exclaimed, when we had swung into the stream and bidden farewell to these men who followed the calling of the apostles, that were she a congressman she would certainly vote for the fisherman's claim, and make happy one more heart in **Grand Detour**.

Now commences the **Great** Bend of the **Rock River.** The water circuit is fourteen miles, the distance gained being but six by land. The stream is broad and shallow, between palisades densely surmounted with trees and covered thick with vines; great willow islands freely intersperse the course; everywhere are evidences of ice-floes, which have blazed the trees and strewn the islands with fallen trunks and driftwood,—a tornado could not have created more general havoc. The visible houses, few of them inviting in appearance, are miles apart. As had been foretold at the village, the outlook for lodgings in this dismal region is not at all encouraging. It was well that we had stopped at Grand Detour.

Below the bend, where the country is more open, though the banks are still deep-cut, the highway to Dixon skirts the river, and for several miles we kept company with the stage.

Dixon was sighted at 10 o'clock. A circus had pitched its tents upon the northern bank, just above the dam, near where we landed for the carry, and a crowd of small boys came swarming down the bank to gaze upon us, possibly imagining, at first, that our outfit was a part of the show. They accompanied us, at a respectful distance, as we pulled the canoe up a grassy incline and down through the vine-clad arches of a picturesque old ruin of a mill. Below the dam, we rowed over to the town, about where the famous pioneer ferry used to be. It was in the spring of 1826 that John Boles opened a trail from Peoria to Galena, by the way of the present locality of Dixon, thus shortening a trail which had been started by one Kellogg the year before, but crossed the Rock a few miles above. The site of Dixon at once sprang into wide popularity as a crossing-place, Indians being employed to do the ferrying. Their manner was simple. Lashing two canoes abreast, the wheels of one side of a wagon were placed in one canoe and the opposite wheels in the other. The horses were made to swim behind. In 1827 a Peoria man named Begordis erected a small shanty here and had half finished a ferry-boat when the Indians, not favoring competition, burned the craft on its stocks and advised Begordis to return to Peoria; being a wise man, he returned. The next year, Joe Ogie, a Frenchman, one of a race that the red men loved, and having a squaw for his wife, was permitted to build a scow, and thenceforth Indians were no longer needed there as common carriers. By the time of the Black Hawk war, Dixon, from whom the subsequent settlement was named, ran the ferry, and the crossing station had henceforth a name in history. A trail in those early days was quite as important as a railroad is to-day; settlements sprang up along the improved "Kellogg's trail," and Dixon was the centre of interest in all northern Illinois. Indeed, it being for years the only point where the river could be crossed by ferry, Dixon was as important a landmark to the settlers of the southern half of Wisconsin who desired to go to Chicago, as any within their own territory.[1]

[1] See Mrs. Kinzie's "Wau-Bun" for a description of the difficulties of travel in "the early day," via Dixon's Ferry.

The Dixon of to-day shelters four thousand inhabitants and has two or three busy mills; although it is noticeable that along the water-power there are some half-dozen mill properties that have been burned, torn down, or deserted, which does not look well for the manufacturing prospects of the place. The land along the river banks is a flat prairie some half-mile in width, with rolling country beyond, sprinkled with oak groves. The banks are of black, sandy loam, from twelve to twenty feet high, based with sandy beaches. The shores are now and then cut with deep ravines, at the mouths of which are fine, gravelly beaches, sometimes forming considerable spits. These indicate that the dry, barren gullies, the gutters of the hillocks, while innocent enough in a drought, sometimes rise to the dignity of torrents and suddenly pour great volumes of drainage into the rapidly filling river,—so often described in the journals of early travelers through this region, as "the dark and raging Rock." This sort of scenery, varied by occasional limestone palisades,—the interesting and picturesque feature of the Rock, from which it derived its name at the hands of the aborigines,—extends down to beyond Sterling.

This city, reached at 3.50 P. M., is a busy

place of ten thousand inhabitants, engaged in miscellaneous manufactures. Our portage was over the south and dry end of the dam. We were helped by three or four bright, intelligent boys, who were themselves carrying over a punt, preparatory to a fishing expedition below. Amid the hundreds of boys whom we met at our various portages, these well-bred Sterling lads were the only ones who even offered their assistance. Very likely, however, the reason may be traced to the fact that this was Saturday, and a school holiday. The boys at the week-day carries were the riff-raff, who are allowed to loaf upon the river-banks when they should be at their school-room desks.

While mechanically pulling a "fisherman's stroke" down stream I was dreamily reflecting upon the necessity of enforced popular education, when W——, vigilant at the steersman's post, mischievously broke in upon the brown study with, "Como's next station! Twenty minutes for supper!"

And sure enough, it was a quarter past six, and there was Como nestled upon the edge of the high prairie-bank. I went up into the hamlet to purchase a quart of milk for supper, and found it a little dead-alive community of perhaps one hundred and twenty-five people.

There is the brick shell of a fire-gutted factory, with several abandoned stores, a dozen houses from which the paint had long since scaled, a rather smart-looking schoolhouse, and two brick dwellings of ancient pattern,— the homes of well-to-do farmers; while here and there were grass-grown depressions, which I was told were once the cellars of houses that had been moved away. On the return to the beach a bevy of open-mouthed women and children accompanied me, plying questions with a simplicity so rare that there was no thought of impertinence. W—— was talking with the old gray-haired ferryman, who had been transporting a team across as we had landed beside his staging. The old man had stayed behind, avowedly to mend his boat, with a stone for a hammer, but it was quite apparent that curiosity kept him, rather than the needs of his scow. He confided to us that Como — which was indeed prettily situated upon a bend of the river — had once been a prosperous town. But the railroad went to some rival place, and — the familiar story — the dam at Como rotted, and the village fell into its present dilapidated state. It is the fate of many a small but ambitious town upon a river. Settled originally because of the river highway, the railroads — that have nearly killed the business of water transportation — did not care to go there because it was too far out of the short-cut path selected by the engineers between two more prominent points. Thus the community is "side-tracked," — to use a bit of railway slang; and a side-tracked town becomes in the new civilization — which cares nothing for the rivers, but clusters along the iron ways — a town "as dead as a door-nail."

We had luncheon on a high bank just out of sight of Como. By the time we had reached a point three or four miles below the village it was growing dark, and time to hunt for shelter. While I walked, or rather ran, along the north bank looking for a farm-house, W—— guided the canoe down a particularly rapid current. It was really too dark to prosecute the search with convenience. I was several times misled by clumps of trees, and fruitlessly climbed over board or crawled under barbed-wire fences, and often stumbled along the dusty highway which at times skirted the bank. It was over a mile before an undoubted windmill appeared, dimly silhouetted against the blackening sky above a dense growth of river-timber a quarter of a mile down the stream. A whistle, and W—— shot the craft into the mouth of a black ravine, and clambered up the bank, at the serious risk of torn clothing from the thicket of blackberry-vines and locust saplings which covered it. Together we emerged upon the highway, determined to seek the windmill on foot; for it would have been impossible to sight the place from the river, which was now, from the overhanging trees on both shores and islands, as dark as a cavern. Just as we stepped upon the narrow road — which we were only able to distinguish because the dust was lighter in color than the vegetation — a farm-team came rumbling along over a neighboring culvert, and rolled into view from behind a fringe of bushes. The horses jumped and snorted as they suddenly sighted our dark forms, and began to plunge. The women gave a mild shriek, and awakened a small child which one of them carried in her arms. I essayed to snatch the bits of the frightened horses to prevent them from running away, for the women had dropped the lines, while W—— called out asking if there was a good farm-house where the windmill was. The team quieted down under a few soothing strokes; but the women persisted in screaming and uttering incoherent imprecations in German, while the child fairly roared. So I returned the lines to the woman in charge, and we bade them "Guten Nacht." As they whipped up their animals and hurried away, with fearful backward glances, it suddenly occurred to us that we had been taken for footpads.

We were so much amused at our adventure, as we walked along, almost groping our way, that we failed to notice a farm-gate on the river side of the road, until a chorus of dogs, just over the fence, arrested our attention. A half-dozen human voices were at once heard calling back the animals. A light shone in thin streaks through a black fringe of lilac-bushes, and in front of these was the gate. Opening the creaky structure, we advanced cautiously up what we felt to be a gravel walk, under an arch of evergreens and lilacs, with the paddle ready as a club, in case of another dog outbreak. But there was no need of it, and we soon emerged into a flood of light, which proceeded from a shadeless lamp within an open window.

It was a spacious white farm-house. Upon the "stoop" of an L were standing, in attitudes of expectancy, a stout, well-fed, though rather sinister-expressioned elderly man, with a long gray beard, and his raw-boned, overworked wife, with two fair but dissatisfied-looking daughters, and several sons, ranging from twelve to twenty years. A few moments of explanation dispelled the suspicious look with which we had been greeted, and it was soon agreed that we should, for a consideration, be entertained for the night and over Sunday; although the good woman protested that her house was "topsy-turvy, all torn up" with house-cleaning,— which excuse, by the way, had become quite familiar by this time, having been current at every house we had thus far entered upon our journey.

Bringing our canoe down to the farmer's bank and hauling it up into the bushes, we returned through the orchard to the house, laden with baggage. Our host proved to be a famous story-teller. His tales, often Munchausenese, were inclined to be ghastly, and he had an o'erweening fondness for inconsequential detail, like some authors of serial tales, who write against space and tax the patience of their readers to its utmost endurance. But while one may skip the dreary pages of the novelist, the circumstantial story-teller must be borne with patiently, though the hours lag with leaden heels. In earlier days the old man had been something of a traveler, having journeyed to Illinois by steamboat on the upper lakes, from "ol' York State;" another time he went down the Mississippi River to Natchez, working his way as a deck

An Ancient Mariner.

hand; but the crowning event of his career was his having, as a driver, accompanied a cattle-train to New York city. A few years ago he tumbled down a well and was hauled up something of a cripple; so that his occupation chiefly consists in sitting around the house in an easy-chair, or entertaining the crowd at the cross-roads store with sturdy tales of his adventures by land and sea, spiced with vigorous opinions on questions of politics and theology. The garrulity of age, a powerful imagination, and a boasting disposition are his chief stock in trade.

Propped up in his great chair, with one leg resting upon a lounge and the other aiding his iron-ferruled cane in pounding the floor by way of punctuating his remarks, "that ancient mariner"

> "Held us with his glittering eye;
> We could not choose but hear."

His tales were chiefly of shooting and stabbing scrapes, drownings and hangings that he claimed to have seen, dwelling upon each incident with a blood-curdling particularity worthy of the reporter of a sensational metropolitan journal. The ancient man must have fairly walked in blood through the greater part of his days; while from the number of corpses that had been fished out of the river, at the head of a certain island at the foot of his orchard, and "laid out" in his best bedroom by the coroner, we began to feel as though we had engaged quarters at a morgue. It was painfully evident that these recitals were "chestnuts" in the house of our entertainer. The poor old lady had a tired-out, unhappy appearance, the dissatisfied-looking daughters yawned, and the sons talked, *sotto voce*, on farm matters and neighborhood gossip.

Finally, we tore away, much to the relief of every one but the host, and were ushered with much ceremony into the ghostly bed-chamber, the scene of so many coroner's inquests. I must confess to uncanny dreams that night, — confused visions of Rock River giving up innumerable corpses, which I was compelled to assist in "laying out" upon the very bed I occupied.

CHAPTER VII.

STORM-BOUND AT ERIE.

WE were somewhat jaded by the time Monday morning came, for Sunday brought not only no relief, but repetitions of many of the most horrible of these "tales of a wayside inn." It was with no slight sense of relief that we paid our modest bill and at last broke away from such ghastly associations. An involuntary shudder overcame me, as we passed the head of the island at the foot of our host's orchard, which he had described as a catch-basin for human floaters.

Our course still lay among large, densely wooded islands, — many of them wholly given up to maples and willows, — and deep cuts through sun-baked mudbanks, the color of adobe; but occasionally there are low, gloomy bottoms, heavily forested, and strewn with flood-wood, while beyond the land rises gradually into prairie stretches. In the bottoms the trees are filled with flocks of birds, — crows, hawks, blackbirds, with stately blue herons and agile plovers foraging on the long gravel-spits which frequently jut far into the stream; ducks are frequently seen sailing near the shores; while divers silently dart and plunge ahead of the canoe, safely out of gunshot reach. A head wind this morning made rowing more difficult, by counteracting the influence of the current.

We were at Lyndon at eleven o'clock. There is a population of about two hundred, clustered around a red paper-mill. The latter made a pretty picture standing out on the bold bank, backed by a number of huge stacks of golden straw. We met here the first rapids worthy of record; also an old, abandoned mill-dam, in the last stages of decay, stretching its whitened skeleton across the stream, a harbor for driftwood. Near the south bank the framework has been entirely swept away for a space several rods in width, and through this opening the pent-up current fiercely sweeps. We went through the centre of the channel thus made, with a swoop that gave us an impetus which soon carried our vessel out of sight of Lyndon and its paper-mill and straw-stacks.

Prophetstown, five miles below, is prettily

situated in an oak grove on the southern bank. Only the gables of a few houses can be seen from the river, whose banks of yellow clay and brown mud are here twenty-five feet high. During the first third of the present century, this place was the site of a Winnebago village, whose chief was White Cloud, a shrewd, sinister savage, half Winnebago and half Sac, who claimed to be a prophet. He was Black Hawk's evil genius during the uprising of 1832, and in many ways was one of the most remarkable aborigines known to Illinois history. It was at "the prophet's town," as White Cloud's village was known in pioneer days, that Black Hawk rested upon his ill-fated journey up the Rock, and from here, at the instigation of the wizard, he bade the United States soldiery defiance.

There are rapids, almost continually, from a mile above Prophetstown to Erie, ten miles below. The river bed here has a sharper descent than customary, and is thickly strewn with bowlders; many of them were visible above the surface, at the low stage of water which we found, but for the greater part they were covered for two or three inches. What with these impediments, the snags that had been left as the legacy of last spring's flood, and the frequent sand-banks and gravel-spits, navigation was attended by many difficulties and some dangers.

Four or five miles below Prophetstown, a lone fisherman, engaged in examining a "traut-line" stretched between one of the numerous gloomy islands and the mainland, kindly informed us of a mile-long cut-off, the mouth of which was now in view, that would save us several miles of rowing. Here, the high banks had receded, with several miles of heavily wooded, boggy bottoms intervening. Floods had held high carnival, and the aspect of the country was wild and deserted. The cut-off was an ugly looking channel; but where our informant had gone through, with his unwieldy hulk, we considered it safe to venture with a canoe, so readily responsive to the slightest paddle-stroke. The current had torn for itself a jagged bed through the heart of a dense and moss-grown forest. It was a scene of howling desolation, rack and ruin upon every hand. The muddy torrent, at a velocity of fully eight miles an hour, went eddying and whirling and darting and roaring among the gnarled and blackened stumps, the prostrate trees, the twisted roots, the huge bowlders which studded its course. The stream was not wide enough for the oars; the paddle was the sole reliance. With eyes strained for obstructions, we turned and twisted through the labyrinth, jumping along at a breakneck speed; and, when we finally rejoined the main river below, were grateful enough, for the run had been filled with continuous possibilities of a disastrous smash-up, miles away from any human habitation.

The thunder-storm which had been threatening since early morning, soon burst upon us with a preliminary wind blast, followed by drenching rain. Running ashore on the lee bank, we wrapped the canvas awning around the baggage, and made for a thick clump of trees on the top of an island mudbank, where we stood buttoned to the neck in rubber coats. A vigorous "Halloo!" came sounding over the water. Looking up, we saw for the first time a small tent on the opposite shore, a quarter of a mile away, in front of which was a man shouting to us and beckoning us over. It was getting uncomfortably muddy under the trees, which had not long sufficed as an umbrella, and the rubber coats were not warranted to withstand a deluge, so we accepted the invitation with alacrity and paddled over through the pelting storm.

Our host was a young fisherman, who helped us and our luggage up the slimy bank to his canvas quarters, which we found to be dry, although odorous of fish. While the storm raged without, the young man, who was a simple-hearted fellow, confided to us the details of his brief career. He had been married but a year, he said; his little cabin lay a quarter of a mile back in the woods, and, so as to be convenient to his lines, he was camping on his own wood-lot; the greater part of his time was spent in fishing or hunting, according to the season, and peddling the product in neighboring towns, while upon a few acres of clearing he raised "garden truck" for his household, which had recently become enriched by the addition of an infant son. The phenomenal powers of observation displayed by this first-born youth were reported with much detail by the fond father, who sat crouched upon a boat-sail in one corner of the little tent, his head between his knees, and smoking vile tobacco in a blackened clay pipe. It seemed that his wife was a ferryman's daughter, and her father had besought his son-in-law to follow the same steady calling. To be sure, our host declared, ferries on the Rock River netted their owners from $400 to $800 a year, which he considered a goodly sum, and his father-in-law had offered to purchase an established plant for him. But the young fellow said that ferrying was a dog's life, and "kept a feller home like barn chores;" he preferred to fish and hunt, earning far less but retaining independence of movement, so rejected the offer and settled down, avowedly for life, in his present precarious occupation. As a result, the indignant old man had forbidden him to again enter the parental ferry-house until he agreed to accept his proposals, and there was henceforth to be a standing family quarrel. The fisherman having appealed to my judgment, I endeavored with mild caution to argue him out of his position on the score of consideration for his wife and little one; but he was not to be gainsaid, and firmly, though with admirable good nature, persisted in defending his roving tendencies. In the course of our conversation I learned that the ferrymen, who are more numerous on the lower than on the upper Rock, pay an annual license fee of five dollars each, in consideration of which they are guarantied a monopoly of the business at their stands, no other line being allowed within one mile of an existing ferry.

Within an hour and a half the storm had apparently passed over, and we continued our journey. But after supper another shower and a stiff head wind came up, and we were well bedraggled by the time a ferry-landing near the little village of Erie was reached. The bottoms are here a mile or two in width, with occasional openings in the woods, where small fields are cultivated by the poorer class of farmers, who were last spring much damaged by the flood which swept this entire country.

The ferryman, a good-natured young athlete, was landing a farm-wagon and team as we pulled in upon the muddy roadway. When questioned about quarters, he smiled and pointing to his little cabin, a few rods off in the bushes, said, — "We've four people to sleep in two rooms; it's sure we can't take ye; I'd like to, otherwise. But Erie's only a mile away."

We assured him that with these muddy swamp roads, and in our wet condition, nothing but absolute necessity would induce us to take a mile's tramp. The parley ended in our being directed to a small farm-house a quarter of a mile inland, where luckless travelers, belated on the dreary bottoms, were occasionally kept. Making the canoe fast for the night, we strung our baggage-packs upon the paddle which we carried between us, and set out along a devious way, through a driving mist which blackened the twilight into dusk, to find this place of public entertainment.

It is a little, one-story, dilapidated farmhouse, standing a short distance from the country road, amid a clump of poplar trees. Forcing our way through the hingeless gate, the violent removal of which threatened the immediate destruction of several lengths of rickety fence, we walked up to the open front door and applied for shelter.

"Yes, ma'am; we sometimes keeps tavern, ma'am," replied a large, greasy-looking, black-haired woman of some forty years, as, her hands folded within her up-turned apron, she courtesied to W——.

We were at once shown into a frowsy apartment which served as parlor, sitting-room and parental dormitory. There was huddled together an odd, slouchy combination of articles of shabby furniture and cheap decorations, peculiar, in the country, to all three classes of rooms, the evidences of poverty, shiftlessness, and untasteful pretentiousness upon every side. A huge, wheezy old cabinet organ was set diagonally in one corner, and upon this, as we entered, a young woman was pounding and paddling with much vigor, while giving us sidelong glances of curiosity. She was a neighbor, on an evening visit, decked out in a smart jockey-cap, with a green ostrich tip and bright blue ribbons, and gay in a new calico dress,— a yellow field thickly planted to purple pineapples. A jaunty, forward creature, in pimples and curls, she rattled away through a Moody and Sankey hymn-book, the wheezes and groans of the antique instrument coming in like mournful ejaculations from the amen corner at a successful revival. Having exhausted her stock of tunes, she wheeled around upon her stool, and after declaring to her half-dozen admiring auditors that her hands were "as tired as after the mornin's milkin'" abruptly accosted W——: "Ma'am, kin ye play on the orgin?"

W—— confessed her inability, chiefly from lack of practice in the art of incessantly working the pedals.

"That's the trick o' the hul business, ma'am, is the blowin'. It's all in gettin' the bellers to work even like. There's a good many what kin learn the playin' part of it without no teacher; but there has to be lessons to learn the bellers. Don't ye have no orgin, when ye're at home?" she asked sharply, as if to guage the social standing of the new guest.

W—— modestly confessed to never having possessed such an instrument.

"Down in these parts," rejoined the young woman, as she "worked the bellers" into a strain or two of "Hold the Fort," apparently to show how easy it came to trained feet, "no house is now considered quite up to the fashi'n as ain't got a orgin." The rain being now over, she soon departed, evidently much disgusted at W——'s lack of organic culture.

The bed-chamber into which we were shown was a marvel. It opened off the main room and was, doubtless, originally a cupboard. Seven feet square, with a broad, roped bedstead occupying the entire length, a bedside space of but two feet wide was left. Much of this being filled with butter firkins, chains, a trunk, and a miscellaneous riff-raff of household lumber, the standing-room was restricted to two feet square, necessitating the use of the bed as a dressing-place, after the fashion of a sleeping-car bunk. This cubby-hole of a room was also the wardrobe for the women of the household, the walls above the bed being hung nearly two feet deep with the oddest collection of calico and gingham gowns, bustles, hoopskirts, hats, bonnets, and winter underwear I think I had ever laid eyes on.

Much of this condition of affairs was not known, however, until next morning; for it was as dark as Egypt within, except for a few faint rays of light which came straggling through the cracks in the board partition separating us from the sitting-room candle. We had no sooner crossed the threshold of our little box than the creaky old cleat door was gently closed upon us and buttoned by our hostess upon the outside, as the only means of keeping it shut; and we were left free to grope about among these mysteries as best we might. We had hardly recovered from our astonishment at thus being locked into a dark hole the size of a fashionable lady's trunk, and were quietly laughing over this odd adventure, when the landlady applied her mouth to a crack and shouted, as if she would have waked the dead: " Hi, there! Ye 'd better shet the winder to keep the bugs out!" A few minutes later, returning to the crack, she added, "Ef ye 's cold in the night, jest haul down some o' them clothes atop o' ye which ye 'll find on the wall."

Repressing our mirth, we assured our good hostess that we would have a due regard for our personal safety. The window, not at first discernible, proved to be a hole in the wall, some two feet square, which brought in little enough fresh air, at the best. It was fortunate that the night was cool, although our hostess's best gowns were not needed to supplement the horse-blankets under which we slept the sleep of weary canoeists.

CHAPTER VIII.

THE LAST DAY OUT.

THE following day opened brightly. We had breakfast in the tavern kitchen, *en famille*. The husband, whom we had not met before, was a short, smooth-faced, voluble, overgrown-boy sort of man. The mother was dumpy, coarse, and good-natured. They had a greasy, easy-tempered daughter of eighteen, with a frowsy head, and a face like a full moon; while the heir of the household, somewhat younger, was a gaping, grinning youth of the Simple Simon order, who shovelled mashed potatoes into his mouth alternately with knife and fork, and took bites of bread large enough for a ravenous dog. The old grandmother, with a face like parchment and one gleaming eye, sat in a low rocking-chair by the stove, crooning over a corn-cob pipe and using the wood-box for a cuspadore. She had a vinegary, slangy tongue, and being somewhat deaf, would break in upon the conversation with remarks sharper than they were pat.

With our host, a glib and rapid talker in a swaggering tone, one could not but be much amused, as he exhibited a degree of self-appreciation that was decidedly refreshing. He had been a veteran in the War of the Rebellion, he proudly assured us, and pointed with his knife to his discharge-paper, which was hung up in an old looking-glass frame by the side of the clock.

"Gemmen,"— he invariably thus addressed us, as though we were a coterie of checker-players at a village grocery, — "Gemmen, when I seen how them Johnny Rebs was a usin' our boys in them prison pens down thar at Andersonville and Libbie and 'roun' thar, I jist says to myself, says I, ' Joe, my boy, you go now an' do some 'n' fer yer country; a crack shot like you is, Joe,' says I to myself, 'as kin hit a duck on the wing, every time, an' no mistake, ought n't ter be a-lyin 'roun' home an' doin' no'hun to put down the rebellion; it's a shame,' says I, ' when our boys is a-suff'r'n' down thar on Mason 'n' Dixie's line;' an' so I jined, an' I stuck her out, gemmen, till the thing was done; they ain't no coward 'bout me, ef I *hev* the sayin' of it!"

"Were you wounded, sir?" asked W——, sympathetically.

"No, I wa'n't hurt at all,— that is, so to speak, wounded. But thar were a sort of a doctor feller 'round here las' winter, a-stoppin' at Erie; an' he called at my place, an' he says, 'No'hun the matter wi' you, a-growin' out o' the war?' says he; an' I says, 'No'hun that I know'd on,' says I, — 'I'm a-eatin' my reg'l'r victuals whin I don't have the shakes,' says I. 'Ah!' says he, 'you've the shakes?' he says; 'an' don't you know you ketched 'em in the war?' 'I ketched 'em a-gettin' m'lairy in the bottoms,' says I, 'a-duck-shootin', in which I kin hit a bird on the wing every time an' no mistake,' says I. 'Now,' he says, 'hold on a minute; you did n't hev shakes afore the war?' says he. 'Not as much,' I says, not knowin' what the feller was drivin' at, 'but some; I was a kid then, and kids don't shake much,' says I. 'Hold up! hold up!' he says, 'you're wrong, an' ye know it; ye don't hev no mem'ry goin' back so far about phys'cal conditions,' says he. Well, gemmen, sure 'nough, when I kem to think things over, and talk it up with the doctor chap, I 'lowed he was right. Then he let on he was a claim agint, an' I let him try his hand on workin' up a pension for me, for he says I wa'n't to pay no'hun 'less the thing went through. But I hearn tell, down at Erie, that they is a-goin' agin these private claims nowadays **at Washin'ton, an'** I don't know what **my** show is. But I ought to hev a pension, **an' no mistake, gemmen. They wa'n't** no fellers did harder work 'n **me** in the war, ef I *do* say it myself."

W—— ventured to **ask** what battles our host had **been in.**

"Well, I wa'n't in no reg'lar battle,—that is, right *in* one. Thar was a few of us detailed ter tek keer of gov'ment prop'ty near C'lumby, South Car'liny, when Wade Hamptin was a-burnin' things down thar. We was four miles away from the fightin',' an' I was jest a-achin' to git in thar. What I wanted was to git a bead on ol' Wade himself,—an' ef I do say it myself, the ol' man would 'a' hunted his hole, gemmen. When I **get a** sight on a duck, gemmen, that duck's mine, an' no mistake. An' ef **I'd 'a'** sighted Wade Hamptin, then good-by Wade! I tol' the cap'n what I wanted, but he said as how **I was** more use a-takin' keer of the supplies. That cap'n had n't no enterprise 'bout him. Things would 'a' been different at C'lumby, ef I'd had my way, an' don't ye forgit it! There was heaps o' blood spilt unnecessary by us boys, a-fightin' to save the ol' flag, — an' we 're willin' to do it agin, gemmen, **an' no** mistake!"

The old woman had been listening eagerly to this narrative, evidently quite proud of **her** boy's achievements, but not hearing all **that** had been said. She now broke out, in shrill, high notes, —

"Joe ought ter 'a' had a pension, he had, wi' his chills 'tracted in the war. He wuk'd hard, Joe did, a hul ten months, doin' calvary **service**, the last year **o'** the war; an' he kem nigh onter shootin' ol' Wade Hamptin, an' a-makin' a name for himself, an' p'r'aps a good **office** with a title an' all that; only they kep' **him** back with the ammernition wagin, 'count **o' the** kurnil's jealousy, — for Joe is a dead shot, ma'am, if I 'm his mother as says it, and keeps the **family in** ducks half the year 'roun', an' the kurnil know'd Joe was a-bilin' over to git to the front."

"Ah! you **were in the** cavalry service, then?" I said to our landlord, by way of helping along the conversation.

There was a momentary silence, broken by Simple Simon, who **wiped his** knife on his tongue, and made a wild attack on the butter **dish.**

"Pa, he druv a mule team for gov'ment;

an' we got a picter in the album, tuk of him when he were just a-goin' inter battle, with a big ammernition wagin on behind. Pa, in the picter, is a-ridin' o' one o' the mules, an' any one 'd know him right off."

This sudden revelation of the strength of the veteran's claim to glory and a pension, put a damper upon his reminiscences of the war; and giving the innocent Simon a savage leer, he soon contrived to turn the conversation upon his wonderful exploits in duck-shooting and fishing — industries in the pursuit of which he, with so many of his fellow-farmers on the bottoms, appeared to be more eager than in tilling the soil.

It was quite evident that the breakfast we were eating was a special spread in honor of probably the only guests the quondam tavern had had these many months. Canoeists must not be too particular about the fare set before them; but on this occasion we were able to swallow but a few mouthfuls of the repast and our lunch-basket was drawn on as soon as we were once more afloat. It is a great pity that so many farmers' wives are the wretched cooks they are. With an abundance of good materials already about them, and rare opportunities for readily acquiring more, tens of thousands of rural dames do

manage to prepare astonishingly inedible meals,
— sour, doughy bread; potatoes which, if
boiled, are but half cooked, and if mashed, are
floated with abominable butter or pastey flour
gravy; salt pork either swimming in a bowl
of grease or fried to a leathery chip; tea
and coffee extremely weak or strong enough
to kill an ox, as chance may dictate, and inevitably adulterated beyond recognition; eggs
that are spoiled by being fried to the consistency of rubber, in a pan of fat deep enough
to float doughnuts; while the biscuits are
yellow and bitter with saleratus. This bill of
fare, warranted to destroy the best of appetites, will be recognized by too many of my
readers as that to be found at the average
American farm-house, although we all doubtless know of some magnificent exceptions,
which only prove the rule. We establish public cooking-schools in our cities, and economists like Edward Atkinson and hygienists
like the late Dio Lewis assiduously explain
to the metropolitan poor their processes of
making a tempting meal out of nothing; but
our most crying need in this country to-day
is a training-school for rural housewives,
where they may be taught to evolve a respectable and economical spread out of the great
abundance with which they are surrounded.

It is no wonder that country boys drift to the cities, where they can obtain properly cooked food and live like rational beings.

The river continues to widen as we approach the junction with the Mississippi, — thirty-nine miles below Erie, — and to assume the characteristics of the great river into which it pours its flood. The islands increase in number and in size, some of them being over a mile in length by a quarter of a mile in breadth; the bottoms frequently resolve themselves into wide morasses, thickly studded with great elms, maples, and cottonwoods, among which the spring flood has wrought direful destruction. The scene becomes peculiarly desolate and mournful, often giving one the impression of being far removed from civilization, threading the course of some hitherto unexplored stream. Penetrate the deep fringe of forest and morass on foot, however, and smiling prairies are found beyond, stretching to the horizon and cut up into prosperous farms. The river is here from a half to three-quarters of a mile broad, but the shallows and snags are as numerous as ever and navigation is continually attended with some danger of being either grounded or capsized.

Now and then the banks become firmer,

with charming vistas of high, wooded hills coming down to the water's edge; broad savannas intervene, decked out with variegated flora, prominent being the elsewhere rare atragene Americana, the spider-wort, the little blue lobelia, and the cup-weed. These savannas are apparently overflowed in times of exceptionally high water; and there are evidences that the stream has occasionally changed its course, through the sunbaked banks of ashy-gray mud, in years long past.

At Cleveland, a staid little village on an open plain, which we reached soon after the dinner-hour, there is an unused mill-dam going to decay. In the centre, the main current has washed out a breadth of three or four rods, through which the pent-up stream rushes with a roar and a hundred whirlpools. It is an ugly crevasse, but a careful examination showed the passage to be feasible, so we retreated an eighth of a mile up-stream, took our bearings, and went through with a speed that nearly took our breath away and appeared to greatly astonish a half-dozen fishermen idly angling from the dilapidated apron on either side. It was like going through Cleveland on the fast mail.

Fourteen miles above the mouth of the Rock, is the Chicago, Burlington and Quincy railroad bridge, with Carbon Cliff on the north and Coloma on the south, each one mile from the river. The day had been dark, with occasional slight showers and a stiff head wind, so that progress had been slow. We began to deem it worth while to inquire about the condition of affairs at the mouth. Under the bridge, sitting on a bowlder at the base of the north abutment, an intelligent-appearing man in a yellow oiled-cloth suit, accompanied by a bright-eyed lad, peacefully fished. Stopping to question them, we found them both well-informed as to the railway time-tables of the vicinity and the topography of the lower river. They told us that the scenery for the next fourteen miles was similar, in its dark desolation, to that which we had passed through during the day; also that owing to the great number of islands and the labyrinth of channels both in the Rock and on the east side of the Mississippi, we should find it practically impossible to know when we had reached the latter; we should doubtless proceed several miles below the mouth of the Rock before we noticed that the current was setting persistently south, and then would have an exceedingly difficult task in retracing our course and pulling up-stream to our destination, Rock Island, which is six miles

north of the delta of the Rock. They strongly
advised our going into Rock Island by rail.
The present landing was the last chance to
strike a railway, except at Milan, twelve miles
below. It was now so late that we could not
hope to reach Milan before dark; there were
no stopping-places *en route*, and Milan was
farther from Rock Island than either Carbon
Cliff or Coloma, with less frequent railway
service.

For these and other reasons, we decided to
accept this advice, and to ship from Coloma.
Taking a final spurt down to a ferry-landing
a quarter of a mile beyond, on the south
bank, we beached our canoe at 5.05 P. M.,
having voyaged two hundred and sixty-seven
miles in somewhat less than seven days and
a half. Leaving W—— to gossip with the
ferryman's wife, who came down to the bank
with an armful of smiling twins, to view a
craft so strange to her vision, I went up into
the country to engage a team to take our
boat upon its last portage. After having
been gruffly refused by a churlish farmer,
who doubtless recognized no difference between a canoeist and a tramp, I struck a bargain with a negro cultivating a cornfield with
a span of coal-black mules, and in half an
hour he was at the ferry-landing with a

wagon. Washing out the canoe and chaining in the oars and paddle, we lifted it into the wagon-box, piled our baggage on top, and set off over the hills and fields to Coloma, W—— and I trudging behind the dray, ankle deep in mud, for the late rains had well moistened the black prairie soil. It was a unique and picturesque procession.

In less than an hour we were in Rock Island, and our canoe was on its way by freight to Portage, preparatory to my tour with our friend the Doctor,—down the Fox River of Green Bay.

THE FOX RIVER (OF GREEN BAY).

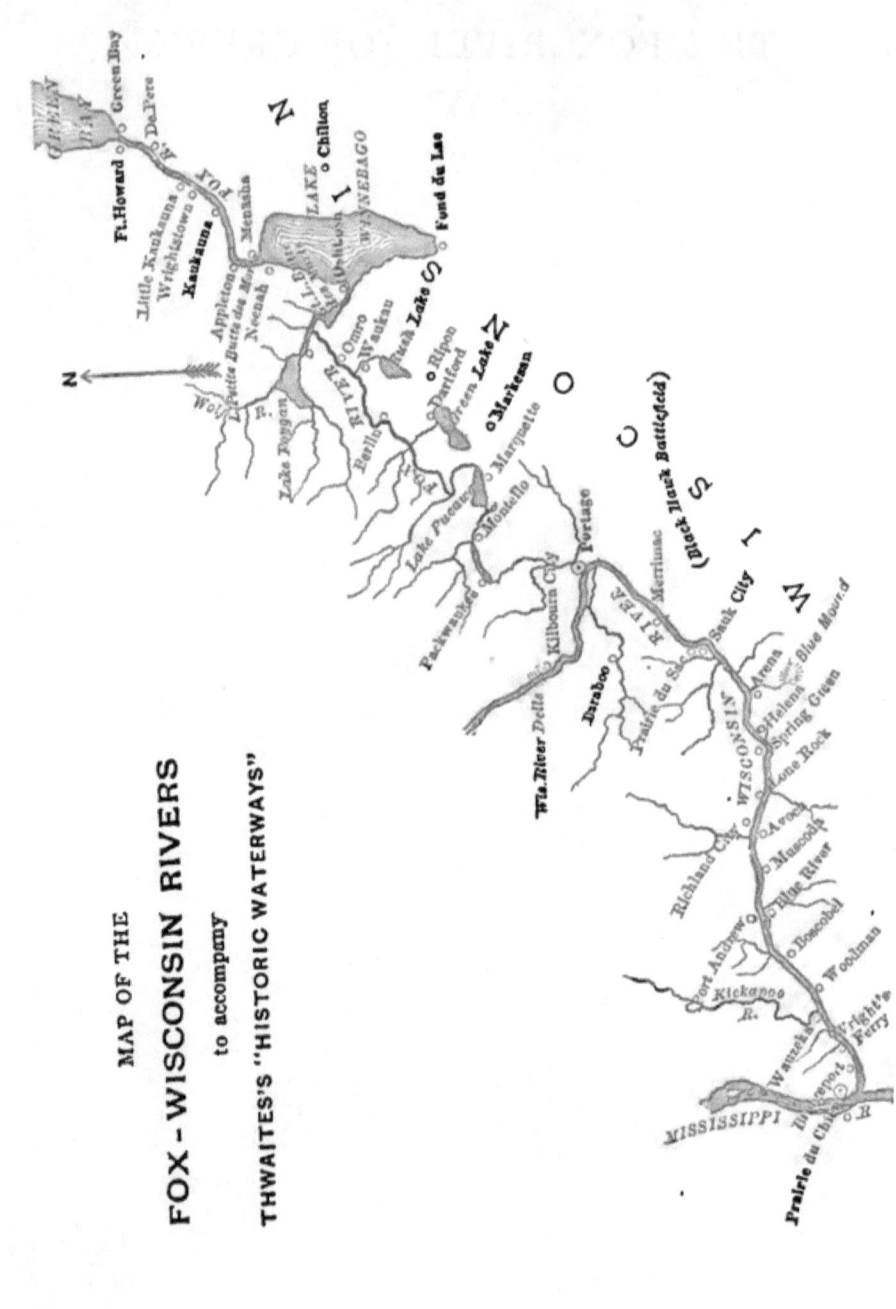

THE FOX RIVER (OF GREEN BAY).

FIRST LETTER.

SMITH'S ISLAND.

PACKWAUKEE, WIS., June 7, 1887.

MY DEAR W——: It was 2.25 P. M. yesterday when the Doctor and I launched the old canoe upon the tan-colored water of the government canal at Portage, and pointed her nose in the direction of the historic Fox. You will remember that the canal traverses the low sandy plain which separates the Fox from the Wisconsin on a line very nearly parallel to where tradition locates Barth's and Lecuyer's wagon-portage a hundred years ago. It was a profitable business in the olden days, when the Fox-Wisconsin highway was extensively patronized, to thus transport river craft over this mile and a half of bog.

The toll[1] collected by these French creoles and their successors down to the days of Paquette added materially to the cost of goods and peltries. In times of exceptionally high water the Wisconsin overflowed into the Fox, which is ordinarily five feet lower than the former, and canoes could readily cross the portage afloat, quite independent of the forwarding agents. In this generation the Wisconsin is kept to her bounds by levees; but the government canal furnishes a free highway. The railroads have spoiled water-navigation, however; and the canal, like the most of the Fox and Wisconsin river-improvement, is fast relapsing into a costly relic. The timbered sides are rotting, the peat and sand are bulging them in, the locks are shaky and worm-eaten, and several moss-covered barges and a stranded old ruin of a steamboat turned out to grass tell a sad story of official abandonment.

The scenic effects from the canal are not enlivening. There is a wide expanse of bog, relieved by some grass-grown railway side-tracks and the forlorn freight-depot of the Wisconsin Central road. A few battered sheds yet remain of old Fort Winnebago on a lonesome hillock near where the

---

[1] Ten dollars per boat, and fifty cents per 100 lbs. of goods.

canal joins the Fox; while beyond to the north as far as the eye can reach there is a stretch of wild-rice swamp, through which the government dredges have scooped a narrow channel, about as picturesque as a cranberry-marsh drain.

Life at Fort Winnebago during the second quarter of this century must have been lonesome indeed, its nearest neighbors being Forts Crawford and Howard, each nearly two hundred miles away. A mile or two to the southwest is a pretty wooded ridge, girting the Wisconsin River, upon which the city of Portage is now situated. Then it was a forest, and the camping-ground of Winnebagoes, who hung around the post in the half-threatening attitude of beggars who might make trouble if not adequately bribed with gifts. The fort was erected in 1828-29 at the solicitation of John Jacob Astor (the American Fur Company), to protect his trade against encroachments from these Winnebago rascals, who had become quite impudent during the Red Bird disturbance at Prairie du Chien, in 1827. Jefferson Davis was one of the three first-lieutenants in the original garrison, in which Harney, of Mexican war fame, was a captain. Davis was detailed to the charge of a squad sent to cut timbers for the fort in a Wisconsin River pinery just above the portage, and thus became one of the pioneer lumbermen of Wisconsin. It is related, too, that Davis, who was an amateur cabinet-maker, designed some very odd wardrobes and other pieces of furniture for the officers' chambers, which were the wonder and admiration of every occupant for years to come.[1] In 1853, when Secretary of War, the whilom subaltern issued an order for the sale of the fort so intimately connected with his army career, and its crazy buildings henceforth became tenements.

For a dozen miles beyond the Fox River end of the canal the river, as I have before said, is dredged out through the swamp like a big ditch. The artificial banks of sand and peat which line it are generally well grown with mare's-tail, beautiful clumps of wild roses, purple vetch, great beds of sensitive ferns, and masses of Pennsylvania anemone, while the pools are decked with water-anemone. Nature is doing her best to hide the deformities wrought by man. The valley is generally about a mile in width, ridges of wooded knolls hemming in the broad expanse of reeds and rice and willow clumps. Occa-

[1] Described in Mrs. Kinzie's "Wau-Bun," which gives many interesting reminiscences of life at the old post.

sionally the engineers have allowed the ditch to swerve in graceful lines and to hug closely the firmer soil in the lower benches of the knolls, where the banks of red and yellow clay attain a height of ten or a dozen feet, crowned with oaks and elms or pleasant glades. A modest farm-house now and then appears upon such a shore, with the front yard running down to the water's edge.

The afternoon shadows are lengthening, and farmers' boys are leading their horses down to drink, after the day's labor in the fields. Black and yellow collies are gathering in the cows, — some of them soberly and quickly corral obedient herds, while others yelp and snap at the heads of the affrighted animals, and in the noise and confusion seem to make but little progress. Collies have human-like infirmities.

We had supper at seven o'clock, under a tree which overhangs a weedy bank, with a high pasture back of us, sloping up to a wooded hill, at the base of which is a cluster of three neatly painted farm-houses, whose dogs bayed at us from the distance, but did not venture to approach. A half-hour later, the sun's setting warned us that quarters for the night must soon be secured. Stopping at the base of a boggy pasture-wood, we ascended through a sterile field, accursed with sheep-sorrel, and through gaps in several crazy fences, to what had seemed to us from the river a comfortable, repose-inviting house, commandingly situated on a hill-top among the trees. Near approach revealed a scene of desolation. The barriers were down, two spare-ribbed horses were nipping a scant supper among the weeds in a dark corner of an otherwise deserted barn-yard, the window-sashes were generally paneless, the porch was in a state of collapse, sand-burrs choked the paths, and to our knock at the kitchen door the only response was a hollow echo. The deserted house looked uncanny in the gloaming, and we retired to our boat wondering what evil spell had been cast over the place, and whether the horses in the barn-yard had been deliberately left behind to die of starvation.

The river now takes upon itself many devious windings in a great widespread over two miles broad. The government engineers have here left it in all its original crookedness, and the twists and turns are as fantastic and complicated as those of the Teutonic pretzel in its native land. As the twilight thickened, great swarms of lake-flies rose from the sedges and beat their way up-stream, the noise of their multitudinous wings being at times like the roar of a neighboring waterfall, as they formed a ceaselessly moving canopy over our heads. It was noticeable that the flies kept very closely to the windings of the river, as if guided only by the glittering flood beneath them. The mass of the procession kept its way up the stream, but upon the outskirts could be seen a few individuals, apparently larger than the average, flying back and forth as if marshaling the host.

Two miles below the deserted house, we stopped opposite another marshy bank, where a rude skiff lay tied to a shaky fence projecting far out into the reeds. Pushing our way in, we beached in the slimy shore-mud and scrambled upon the land, where the tall grass was now as sloppy with dew as though it had been rained upon. It was getting quite dark now, but through a cleft in the hills the moon was seen to be just rising above a cloud-bathed horizon, and a small house, neat-looking, though destitute of paint, was sharply silhouetted against the lightening sky, at the head of a gentle slope. By the time we had waded through a quarter of a mile of thriving timothy we were wet to the skin below the knees and dusted all over with pollen.

Seven children, mostly boys, and gently step-laddered down from fourteen years, greeted us at the summit with a loud "Hello!" in shrill unison. They stood in a huddle by the woodpile, holding down and admonishing a very mild-looking collie, which they evidently imagined was filled with an overweening desire instantly to devour us. "Hello there! who be ye?" shouted the oldest lad and the spokesman of the party. He was a tall, spare boy, and by the light of the rising moon we could see he was sharp-featured, good-natured, and intelligent.

"Well," said the Doctor, bantering, "that's what we'd like to know. You tell us who you are, and we'll tell you who we are. Now that's fair, is n't it?"

"Yes, sir," replied the boy, respectfully, as he touched his rimless straw hat; "our name's Smith; all 'cept that boy there," pointing to a sturdy little twelve-year-old, "an' he's a Bixby, he is."

"The Smith family's a big one, I should say," the Doctor remarked, as he audibly counted the party.

"Oh, this ain't all on 'em, sir; there's two in the house, a-hidin' 'cause o' strangers, besides the baby, which ma and pa has with 'em inter Packwaukee, a-shoppin'. This is Smith's Island, sir. Did n't ye ever hear o' Smith's Island?"

We acknowledged our ignorance, up to this time, of the existence of any such feature in the geography of Wisconsin. But the lad, now joined by the others, who had by this time vanquished their bashfulness and all wanted to talk at once, assured us that we were actually on Smith's Island; that Smith's Island had an area of one hundred acres, was surrounded on the east by the river, and everywhere else by either a bayou or a marsh that had to be crossed with a boat in the spring; that there were three families of Smiths there, and this group represented but one branch of the clan.

"We're all Smiths, sir, but this boy, who's a Bixby; an' he's our cousin and only a-visitin'."

After having gained a thorough knowledge of the topography and population of Smith's Island, we ventured to ask whether it was presumable that the parental Smiths, when they returned home from the village, would be willing to entertain us for the night.

"Guess not, sir," replied the spokesman, the idea appearing to strike him humorously; "there's so many of us now, sir, that we're packed in pretty close, an' the Bixby boy has to sleep atop o' the orgin. But I think Uncle Jim might; he kept a tramp over night once, an' give him his breakfus', too, in the bargain."

The prospect as to Uncle Jim was certainly encouraging, and it was now too late to go further. It seemed necessary to stop on Smith's Island for the night, even if we were restricted to quartering in the corn-crib which the Smith boy kindly put at our disposal in case of Uncle Jim's refusal, — with the additional inducement that he would lend us the collie for company and to "keep off rats," which he intimated were phenomenally numerous on this swamp-girt hill.

The entire troop of urchins accompanied us down to the bank to make fast for the night, and helped us up with our baggage to the corn-crib, where we disturbed a large family of hens which were using the airy structure as a summer dormitory. Then, with the two oldest boys as pilots, we set off along the ridge to find the domicile of Uncle Jim, who had established a reputation for hospitality by having once entertained a way-worn tramp.

The moon had now swung clear of the trees on the edge of the river basin, and gleamed through a great cleft in the blue-black clouds, investing the landscape with a luminous glow. Along the eastern horizon a dark forest-girt ridge hemmed in the reedy widespread, through which the gleaming Fox twisted and doubled upon itself like a silvery serpent in agony. **The** Indians, who have an eye to the picturesque in Nature, **tell us that** once a monster snake lay down for the night **in the swamp** between the portage and the lake of the Winnebagoes. The dew accumulated upon it as it lay, and when the morning came it wriggled and shook the water from its back, and disappeared down the river which it had thus created in its nocturnal **bed.** I had never fully appreciated the aptness of the legend until last night, when I had that bird's-eye view of the valley of the Fox from the summit of Smith's Island. **To our** left, the timothy-field sloped gracefully down to the sedgy couch of the serpent; to our right, **there** were pastures and oak openings, with glimpses of the moonlit bayou below, across which **a** dark line led to a forest,—the narrow roadway leading from Smith's to the outer world. At the edge of a small wood-lot our guides stopped, telling us to keep on along the path, over two stiles and through a barn-yard gate, till we saw a light; the light would be Uncle Jim's.

A cloud was by this time overcasting the moon, and a distant rumble told us that the night would be stormy. Groping our way through the copse, we passed the barriers, and, according to promise, the blinding light of a kerosene lamp standing on the ledge of an open window burst upon us. Then a door opened, and the form of a tall, stalwart man stood upon the threshold, a striking silhouette. It was Uncle Jim peering into the darkness, for he had heard footsteps in the yard. We were greeted cordially on the porch, and shown into a cosey sitting-room, where Uncle Jim had been reading his weekly paper, and Uncle Jim's wife, smiling sweetly amid her curl-papers, was engaged on a bit of crochet. Charmingly hospitable people they are. They have been married but a year or two, are without children, and have a pleasant cottage furnished simply but in excellent taste. Such delightful little homes are rare in the country, and the Doctor could n't help telling Uncle Jim so, whereat the latter was very properly pleased. Uncle Jim is a fine-looking, manly fellow, six feet two in his stockings, he told us; and his pretty, blooming wife, though young, has the fine manners of the olden school. We were earnestly invited to stop for the night before we had fairly stated our case, and in five minutes were talking on politics, general news, and agriculture, as though we had always lived on

Smith's Island and had just dropped in for an evening's chat. I am sure you would have enjoyed it, W——, it was such a contrast to our night at the Erie tavern, — only a week ago, though it seems a month. One sees and feels so much, canoeing, that the days are like weeks of ordinary travel. Two hundred miles by river are more full of the essence of life than two thousand by rail.

We had an excellent bed and an appetizing breakfast. The flood-gates of heaven had been opened during the night, and Smith's Island shaken to its peaty foundations by great thunder-peals. Uncle Jim was happy, for the pasturage would be improved, and the corn crop would have a "show." Uncle Jim's wife said there would now be milk enough to make butter for market; and the hens would do better, for somehow they never would lay regularly during the drought we had been experiencing. And so we talked on while the "clearing showers" lasted. I told Uncle Jim that I was surprised to see him raising anything at all in what was apparently sand. He acknowledged that the soil was light, and inclined to blow away on the slightest aerial provocation, but he nevertheless managed to get twenty bushels of wheat to the acre, and the lowlands gave him an abundance of hay and pasturage. He was decidedly in favor of mixed crops, himself, and was gradually getting into the stock line, as he wanted a crop that could "walk itself into market." The Doctor inquired about the health of the neighborhood, which he found to be excellent. He is much of a gallant, you know; and Uncle Jim's wife was pleasantly flustered when, in his most winning tones, the disciple of Æsculapius declared that the climate that could produce such splendid complexions as hers — and Uncle Jim's — must indeed be rated as available for a sanitarium.

By a quarter to eight o'clock this morning the storm had ceased, and the eastern sky brightened. Our kind friends bade us a cheery farewell, we retraced our steps to the corn-crib, the Smith boys helped us down with our load, and just as our watches touched eight we shoved off into the stream, and were once more afloat upon the serpentine trail.

These great wild-rice widespreads — sloughs, the natives call them — are doubtless the beds of ancient lakes. In coursing through them, the bayous, the cul-de-sacs, are so frequent, and the stream switches off upon such unexpected tangents, that it is sometimes perplexing to ascertain which body of sluggish water is the main channel. Marquette found this out when he ascended the Fox in 1673. He says, in his relation of the voyage, "The way is so cut up by marshes and little lakes that it is easy to go astray, especially as the river is so covered with wild oats [wild rice] that you can hardly discover the channel; hence, we had good need of our two guides."

Little bog-islands, heavily grown with aspens and willows, occasionally dot the seas of rice. They often fairly hum with the varied notes of the red-winged blackbird, the rusty grackle, and our American robin, while whistling plovers are seen upon the mud-spits, snapping up the choicest of the snails. And such bullfrogs! I have not heard their like since, when a boy, living on the verge of a New England pond, I imagined their hollow rumble of a roundelay to bear the burden of "Paddy, go 'round! Go 'round and 'round!" This in accordance with a local tradition which says that Paddy, coming home one night o'erfull of the " craithur," came to the edge of the pond, which stopped his progress. The friendly frogs, who themselves enjoy a soaking, advised him to go around the obstruction; and as the wild refrain kept on, Paddy did indeed " go 'round, and 'round " till morning and his better-half found him, a foot-sore and a soberer man. They tell us that on the Fox River the frogs say, "Judge Arndt! Arndt! Judge Arndt!" Old Judge Arndt was one of the celebrities in the early day at Green Bay; he was a fur-trader, and accustomed, with his gang of *voyageurs*, to navigate the Fox and Wisconsin with heavily laden canoes and Mackinaw boats. A Frenchman, he had a gastronomic affection for frogs' legs, and many a branch of the house of Rana was cast into mourning in the neighborhood of his nightly camps. The story goes, therefore, that unto this time whenever a boat is seen upon the river, sentinel frogs give out the signal cry of "Judge Arndt!" by way of deadly warning to their kind. Certain it is that the valley of the upper Fox, by day or by night, is resonant with the bellow of the amphibious bull. It is not always "Judge Arndt!" but occasionally, as if miles and miles away, one hears a sudden twanging note, like that of the finger-snapped bass string of a violin; whereas the customary refrain may be likened to the deep reverberations of the bass-viol. Add the countless chatter and whistle of the birds, the ear-piercing hum of the cicada, and the muffled chimes from scores of sheep and cow bells on the hillside pastures, and we have an orchestral accompaniment upon our voyage that could be fully appreciated only in a Chinese theatre.

In the pockets and the sloughs, we find thousands of yellow and white water-lilies, and sometimes progress is impeded by masses of creeping root-stalks which have been torn from their muddy bed by the upheaval of the ice, and now float about in great rafts, firmly anchored by the few whose extremities are still imbedded in the ooze.

Fishing-boats were also occasionally met with this morning, occupied by Packwaukee people; for in the widespreads just above this village, the pickerel thrives mightily off the swarms of perch who love these reedy seas; and the weighty sturgeon often swallows a hook and gives his captor many a frenzied tug before he consents to enter the "live-box" which floats behind each craft.

SECOND LETTER.

FROM PACKWAUKEE TO BERLIN.

BERLIN, WIS., June 8, 1887.

MY DEAR W——: Packwaukee is twenty-five miles by river below Portage, and at the head of Buffalo Lake. It is a tumble-down little place, with about one hundred inhabitants, half of whom appeared to be engaged in fishing. A branch of the Wisconsin Central Railway, running south from Stevens Point to Portage, passes through the town, with a spur track running along the north shore of the lake to Montello, seven miles east. Regular trains stop at Packwaukee, while the engine draws a pony train out to Montello to pick up the custom of that thriving village. Packwaukee apparently had great pretensions once, with her battlement-fronts and verandaed inn; but that day has long passed, and a picturesque float-bridge, mossy and decayed, remains the sole point of artistic interest. A dozen boys were angling from its battered hand-rail, as we painfully crept with our craft through a small tunnel where the abutment had been washed out by the stream. We emerged covered with cobwebs and sawdust, to be met by boys eagerly soliciting us to purchase their fish. The Doctor, somewhat annoyed by their pertinacity as he vigorously dusted himself with his handkerchief, declared, in the vernacular of the river, that we were " clean busted ;" and I have no doubt the lads believed his mild fib, for we looked just then as though we had seen hard times in our day.

Our general course had hitherto been northward, but was now eastward for a few miles and afterward southeastward as far as Marquette. Buffalo Lake is seven miles long by from a third to three quarters of a mile broad. The banks are for the most part sandy, and from five to fifty feet high. The river here merely fills its bed; being deeper, the wild rice and reeds do not grow upon its skirts. Were there a half-dozen more feet of water, the Fox would be a chain of lakes from Portage to Oshkosh. As it is, we have Buffalo, Puckawa, and Grand Butte des Morts, which are among the prettiest of the inland seas of Wisconsin. The knolls about Buffalo Lake are pleasant, round-topped elevations, for the most part wooded, and between them are little prairies, generally sandy, but occasionally covered with dark loam.

The day had, by noon, developed into one of the hottest of the season. The run down Buffalo Lake was a torrid experience long to be remembered. The air was motionless, the sky without clouds; we had good need of our awning. The Doctor, who is always experimenting, picked up a flat stone on the beach, so warm as to burn his fingers, and tried to fry an egg upon it by simple solar heat, but the venture failed and a burning-glass was needed to complete the operation.

Montello occupies a position at the foot of the lake, commanding the entire sheet of water. The knoll upon which the village is for the most part built is nearly one hundred feet high, and the simple spire of an old white church pitched upon the summit is a landmark readily discernible in Packwaukee, seven miles distant. There is a government lock at Montello, and a small water-power. A levee protects from overflow a portion of the town which is situated somewhat below the lake level. The government pays the lock-keepers thirty dollars per month for about eight months in the year, and house-rent the year round.

Tollage is no longer required, and the keepers are obliged by the regulations of the engineering department to open the gates for all comers, even a saw-log. But the services of the keepers are so seldom required in these days that we find they are not to be easily roused from their slumbers, and it is easier and quicker to make the portage at the average up-river lock. Our carry at Montello was two and a half rods, over a sandy bank, where a solitary small boy, who had been catching crayfish with a dip-net, carefully examined our outfit and propounded the inquiry, "Be you fellers on the guv'ment job?"

Below the lock for three or four miles, the river is again a mere canal, but the rigid banks of dredge-trash are for the most part covered with a thrifty vegetation, and have assumed charms of their own. This stage passed, and the river resumes a natural appearance, — a placid stream, with now and then a slough, or perhaps banks of peat and sand, ten feet high and fairly well hung with trees and shrubs.

As we approach the head of Lake Puckawa, the widespreads broaden, with rows of hills two or three miles back, on either side, — the river mowing a narrow swath through the expanse of reeds and flags and rice which unites their bases. Where the widespread becomes a pond, and the lake commences, there is a sandbar, the dregs of the upper channel. A government dredge-machine was at work, cutting out a water-way through the obstruction, — or, rather, had been at work, for it was seven o'clock by this time, the men had finished their supper, and were enjoying themselves upon the neat deck of the boarding-house barge, in a neighboring bayou, smoking their pipes and reading newspapers. It was a comfortable picture.

A stern-wheel freight steamer, big and cumbersome, came slowly into the mouth of the channel as we left it, bound up, for Montello. As we glided along her side, a safe distance from the great wheelbarrow paddle, she loomed above us, dark and awesome, like a whale overlooking a minnow. It was the "T. S. Chittenden," wood-laden. The "Chittenden" and the "Ellen Hardy" are the only boats navigating the upper Fox this season, above Berlin. Their trips are supposed to be semi-weekly, but as a matter of fact they dodge around, all the way from Winneconne to Montello, picking up what freight they can and making a through trip perhaps once a week. It is poor picking, I am told, and the profits but barely pay for maintaining the service.

There now being no place to land, without the great labor of poling the canoe through the dense reed swamp to the sides, we had supper on board, — the Doctor deftly spreading a bit of canvas on the bottom between us, for a cloth, and attractively displaying our lunch to the best advantage. I leisurely paddled meanwhile, occasionally resting to take a mouthful or to sip of the lemonade, in the preparation of which the Doctor is such an adept. And thus we drifted down Lake Puckawa, amid the delightful sunset glow and the long twilight which followed, — the Doctor, cake in one hand and a glass of lemonade in the other, becoming quite animated in a detailed description of a patient he had seen in a Vienna hospital, whose food was introduced through a slit in his throat. The Doctor is an enthusiast in his profession, and would stop to advise St. Peter, at the gate, to try his method for treating locksmith-palsy.

We noticed a great number of black terns as we progressed, perched upon snags at the head of the lake. They are fearless birds, and would allow us to drift within paddle's length before they would rise and, slowly wheeling around our heads, settle again upon their roosts, as soon as we had passed on.

Lake Puckawa is eight miles long by perhaps two miles wide, running west and east. Five miles down the eastern shore, the quaint little village of Marquette is situated on a pleasant slope which overlooks the lake from end to end. Marquette is on the site of an Indian fur-trading camp, this lake being for many years a favorite resort of the Winnebagoes. There are about three hundred inhabitants there, and it is something of a mystery as to how they all scratch a living; for the town is dying, if not already dead,— about the only bit of life noticeable there being a rather pretty club-house owned by a party of Chicago gentlemen, who come to Lake Puckawa twice a year to shoot ducks, it being one of the best sporting-grounds in the State. That is to say, they have heretofore come twice a year, but the villagers were bewailing the passage by the legislature, last winter, of a bill prohibiting spring shooting, thus cutting off the business of Marquette by one half. Marquette, like so many other dead river-towns, appears to have been at one time a community of some importance. There are two deserted saw-mills and two or three abandoned warehouses, all boarded up and falling into decay, while nearly every store-building in the place has shutters nailed over the windows, and a once substantial sidewalk has become such a rotten snare that the natives use the grass-grown street for a footpath. The good people are so tenacious of the rights of visiting sportsmen that there is no angling, I was told, except by visitors, and we inquired in vain for fish at the dilapidated little hotel where we slept and breakfasted. At the hostlery we were welcomed **with** open arms, and the landlady's boy, who officiated as clerk, porter, and chambermaid, assured us that the village schoolmaster had been the only guest for six weeks past.

It is certainly a quiet spot. The Doctor, who knows all about these things, diagnosed the lake and declared **it to** be a fine field for fly-fishing. He had waxed so enthusiastic over the numbers of nesting ducks which we disturbed as we came down through the reeds, in the early evening, that I had all I could do to keep him from breaking the new game law, although he stoutly declared that revolvers did n't count. The postmaster — a pleasant old gentleman in spectacles, who also keeps the drug store, deals in ammunition, groceries, and shoes, and is an agent for agricultural machinery — got very friendly with the Doctor, and confided to him the fact that if the latter would come next fall to Markesan, ten miles distant, over the sands, and telephone up that he was there, a team would be sent down for him ; then, with the postmaster for a guide, fish and fowl would soon be obliged to seek cover. It is needless to add that the Doctor struck a bargain with the postmaster and promised to be on hand without fail. I never saw our good friend so wild with delight, and the postmaster became as happy as if he had just concluded a cash contract for a car-load of ammunition.

The schoolmaster, a very accommodating young man, helped us down to the beach this morning with our load. Anticipating numerous lakes and widespreads, where we might gain advantage of the wind, we had brought a sprit sail along, together with a temporary keel. The sail helped us frequently yesterday, especially in Buffalo Lake, but the wind had died down after we passed Montello. This morning, however, there was a good breeze again, but quartering, and the keel became essential. This we now attached to our craft, and it was nearly seven o'clock before we were off, although we had had breakfast at 5.30.

The "Ellen Hardy" was at the dock, loading with wheat for Princeton. She is a trimmer, faster craft than the "Chittenden." The engineer told us that the present stage of water was but two and a half feet in the upper Fox, this year and last being the driest on record. He informed us that the freight business was "having the spots knocked off it" by the railroads, and there was hardly enough to make it worth while getting up steam.

Three miles down is the mouth of the lake. There being two outlets around a large marsh, we were somewhat confused in trying to find the proper channel. We ascertained, after going a mile and a half out of our way to the south, that the northern extremity of the marsh is the one to steer for. The river continues to wind along between marshy shores, although occasionally hugging a high bank of red clay or skirting a knoll of shifting sand; now and then these knolls rise to the dignity of hills, red with sorrel and sparsely covered with scrubby pines and oaks.

It was noon when we reached the lock above Princeton. The lock-keeper, a remarkably round-shouldered German, is a pleasant, gossipy fellow, fond of his long pipe and his very fat frau. Upon invitation, we made ourselves quite at home in the lock-house, a pleasant little brick structure in a plot of made land, the entire establishment having that rather stiffly neat, ship-shape appearance peculiar to life-saving stations, navy-yards, and military barracks. The good frau steeped for us a pot of tea, and in other ways helped us to grace our dinner, which we spread on a bench under a grape arbor, by the side of the yawning stone basin of the lock.

The "Ellen Hardy," which had left Marquette nearly an hour later than we, came along while we were at dinner, waking the echoes with three prolonged steam groans. We took advantage of the circumstance to lock through in her company. This was our first experience of the sort, so we were naturally rather timid as we brushed her great paddle, going in, and stole along under her overhanging deck, for she quite filled the lock. The captain kindly allowed the liliputian to glide through in advance of his steamer, however, when the gates were once more opened, and we felt, as we shot out, as though we had emerged from under the belly of a monster.

Beaching again, below the lock, we returned to finish our dinner. The keeper asked for a ride to Princeton village, three miles below, and we admitted him to our circle, — pipe, market-basket and all, though it caused the canoe to sink uncomfortably near to the gunwale. Going down, our voluble friend talked very freely about his affairs. He said that his pay of $30 per month ran from about the middle of April to the first of December, and averaged him, the year round, about $20 and house-rent. He had but little to do, and got along very comfortably on the twenty-five acres of marsh-land which the government owned, by raising pigs and cows, a few vegetables, and hay enough for his stock. He admitted that this was "a heap better" than he could do in the fatherland.

"I shoost dell you, mine frient," he said to me, as he grinned and refilled his pipe, "dot Shermany vos a nice guntry, and Bismarck he vos a grade feller, und I vos brout **I vos a** Sherman ; but I dells mine vooman vot I dells you, — I mooch rahder read aboud 'em in mine Sherman newsbaper, dan vot I voot leef dere myself, already. I roon avay vrom dem conscrip' fellers, und I shoost never seed de time vot I voot go back again. In dot ol' guntry, I vos nuttings boot a beasant feller ; unt in dis guntry I vos a goov'ment off'cer, vich makes grade diff'rence, already."

He chuckled a good deal to himself when asked what he thought about the Fox-Wisconsin river-improvement, but finally said that government must spend its surplus some way, — if not in this, it would in another, — and he could not object to a scheme which gave him his bread and butter. He said that the improvement operations scattered a good deal of money throughout the valley, for labor and supplies, but expressed his doubts as to the ultimate national value of the work, unless the shifting Wisconsin River, thus far unnavigable for steamers, should be canalled from the portage to its mouth. He is an honest fellow, and appears to utilize his abundance of leisure in reading the newspapers.

At Princeton village, — a thriving country town on a steep bank, with unkempt backyards running down to and defiling the river, — we again came across the "Ellen Hardy." She was unloading her light cargo of wheat as we arrived, and left Princeton an eighth of a mile behind us. We now had a pleasant little race to White River lock, seven miles below. With sail set, and paddles to help, we led her easily as far as the lock. But we thought to gain time by portaging over the dam, and she gained a lead of at least a mile, although we frequently caught sight of her towering white hull across the widespreads, by dint of standing on the thwarts and peering over the tall walls of wild rice which shut us in as closely as though we had been canoeing in a railroad cut.

It had been fair and cloudy by turns to-day, but delightfully cool, — a wonderful improvement on yesterday, when we fairly sweltered, coming down Buffalo Lake. In the middle of the afternoon, below White River, a thunderstorm overtook us in a widespread several miles in extent. Seeking a willow island which abutted on the channel, we made a tent of the sail and stood the brief storm quite comfortably. We then pushed on, and, rubber-coated, weathered the few clearing showers in the boat, for we were anxious to reach Berlin by evening.

At Berlin lock, twelve miles below White River, we portaged the dam, and, getting into a two-mile current, ate our supper on board. The river now begins to have firmer banks, and to approach the ridges upon the southern rim of its basin.

We reached Berlin in the twilight, the landscape of hill and meadow being softened in the golden glow. The better portion of this beautiful little city of forty-five hundred inhabitants is situated on a ridge, closely skirted by the river, with the poorer quarters on the flats spreading away on either side. There are many charming homes and the main business street has an air of active prosperity.

We went into dock alongside of the "Ellen Hardy."

THIRD LETTER.

THE MASCOUTINS.

Oshkosh, Wis., June 9, 1887.

MY DEAR W——: As we passed out of Berlin this morning, a government dredger was at work by the river-side. We paused on our paddles for some time, to watch the workings of the ingenious mechanism. There was something demoniac in the action of the monster, as it craned its jointed neck amid a quick chorus of jerky puffs from the engine and an accompaniment of rattling chains. Reaching far out over the bubbling water, it would open its great iron jaws with a savage clank and, pausing a moment to gather its energies, dive swiftly into the roily depth; after swaying to and fro as if struggling with its prey, it soon reappeared, bearing in its filthy maw a ton or two of blue-black ooze, the water escaping through its teeth in a score of hissing torrents ; then, turning aside to the heap of dredge-trash, suddenly vomited forth the foul-smelling mess, and returned for another charge. It was a singularly fascinating sight, though wofully uncanny.

From Berlin down to Omro, pleasant prairie slopes come down at intervals to the water's edge, on the south bank ; the feature of the north side being wide expanses of bog, the home of the cranberry, for which this region is famous. The best marshes, however, are the pockets, back among the ridges ; from these, great drainage-ditches, with flooding gates, come furrowing through the peat, in dark lines as straight as an arrow, and empty into the river. It was somewhere about here, nearer Berlin than Omro, — but exactly where, no man now knoweth, — that the ancient Indian "nation" of the Mascoutins was located over two centuries ago ; their neighbors, if not their village comrades, being the Miamis and the Kickapoos. Champlain, the intrepid founder of Quebec, had heard of their warring disposition as early as 1615. In 1634 Jean Nicolet, the first white man known to have set foot upon territory now included in the State of Wisconsin, came in a **bark canoe** as far up the Fox River as the Mascoutins, and after stopping **a** time with them, journeyed southward to the country of the Illinois.[1] Allouez and his companions also came hither in 1670, and the good father, in the official report of his adventurous canoeing trip, says the fort of these people was located a French league (2.4 English miles) "over beautiful prairies" to the south of the river. Joliet and Marquette, on their way to discover the Mississippi River, arrived at the fort of the Mascoutins on June 7, 1673, and the latter gives this graceful sketch of the oak openings hereabouts, which have not meanwhile perceptibly changed their characteristics: "I felt no little pleasure in beholding the position of this town; the view is beautiful and very picturesque, for from the eminence on which it is perched, the eye discovers on every side prairies spreading away beyond its reach, interspersed with thickets or groves of lofty trees."

The Mascoutins are now a lost tribe. As the result of warring habits, they in turn were crowded to the wall, and a generation after Marquette's visit the banks of their river knew them no more; the Foxes, from whom the stream ultimately took its name, were then predominant, and long continued the masters of the highway.

[1] Butterfield's "Discovery of the Northwest" (Cincinnati, 1861).

Sacramento — "as dead as a door-nail, sir" — lies sprawled out over a pleasant riverside slope to the south. There is the customary air of fallen grandeur at Sacramento, — big hopes gone **to decay; battle**ment-fronts, houseless cellars, a universal lack of paint. The railroads, the real highways of our present civilization, have killed these little river towns that are away from the track, and they will never be resurrected. The day of inland water navigation, except for canoeists, is nearing its close. Settlement clings to the neighborhood of the rails, and generally avoids rivers as an obstruction to free transit. The towns that have to be reached by a country **ferry are ro**tting, — they are off the line of progress. Sacramento boasts a spouting well by the river-bank, a mammoth village ash-leach, and fond memories of the day when it was " a bigger **town** than Berlin." As we stood in the spray of the fountain, filling our canteen with the purest and coldest of water, I speculated upon the strong probability of Sacramento being on the identical bank where the Jesuits beached their canoes to walk across country to the old Indian village. And the Doctor, apt to be irreverent as to aboriginal lore, suggested that the defunct Sacramento should have written over its gate this motto: "Gone to join the Mascoutins!"

Eureka, a few miles farther down, is also paintless, and her river-front is artistic with the crumbling ruins of two or three long-deserted saw-mills. A new Eureka appears, however, to be slowly building up, to one side of the dead little hamlet, — for there are smart steam flouring-mill and a model little cheese-factory in full swing here. The cheese man, an accommodating young fellow who appeared quite up to the times, and is a direct shipper to the London market, took a just pride in showing us over his establishment, and stocked our mess-box with samples of his best brands.

Omro spreads over a sandy plain, upon both sides of the river, — an excellent wagon-bridge crossing the stream near that of the Chicago, Milwaukee, and St. Paul railway. Omro, which is the headquarters of the Wisconsin Spiritualists, who have quite a settlement hereabouts, is growing somewhat, after a long period of stagnation, having at present a population of fifteen hundred.

The "Ellen Hardy," which had now caught up with us, after chasing the canoe from Berlin down, went through the draw in our company. As the crew rolled off a small consignment of freight, the captain — a raw-boned, red-faced, and thoroughly good-humored man — leaned out of the pilot-house window and pleasantly chaffed us about our lowly conveyance. The conversation ended by his offering to give us a "lift" through the great Winneconne widespread, to the point where the Wolf joins the Fox, nine or ten miles below. The "Ellen" was bound for Winneconne and other points up the Wolf, so could help us no farther. Of course we accepted the kindly offer, and fastening our painter to a belaying-pin on the "Ellen's" port, scrambled up to the freight-deck just as the pilot-bell rang "Forward!" in the smoky little engine-room far aft.

While I went aloft to enjoy the bird's-eye view obtainable from the pilot-house, the Doctor discussed fishing with the engineer, whom he found on closer acquaintance to be a rare, though much-begrimed philosopher. This engineer is a wizened-up little man, with a face like a prematurely dried apple, but his eyes gleam with a kindly light, and he is an inveterate angler. We had noticed him at every stopping stage, — his head, shoulders, and arms reaching out of the abbreviated rear window of his caboose, — dangling a line astern. The Doctor learned that this was his invariable habit. He kept the cook's galley in fish, and utilized each leisure half-hour in the pursuit of his favorite amusement. The engineer, good man, had fished, he said, in nearly every known sea, and the Doctor declared that he "could many a wondrous fish-tale unfold." In fact, the Doctor declared him to be the most interesting character he had ever met with, outside of a hospital, and said he should surely report to his favorite medical journal this remarkable case of abnormal persistency in an art, amid the most discouraging physical surroundings. He thought the man's brain should be dissected, in the cause of science.

The Wolf, which has its rise 150 miles nor'-nor'west of Green Bay, in a Forest-county lakelet, and takes generous, south-trending curves away down to Lake Poygan, is properly the noble stream which pours into Lake Winnebago from the northwest, and then, with a mighty rush, forces its way northeastward to the Great Lakes, along the base of the watershed which parallels the western coast of Lake Michigan and terminates in the sands of the Sturgeon-Bay country. The Jesuit fathers, in seeking the Mississippi, traced this river above Lake Winnebago, and on reaching the great widespread at the head of the Grand Butte des Morts, where the tributary flowing from the southwest empties its lazy flood into the rushing Fox, pursued that tributary **to the** portage and erroneously called their highway by one name, from Green Bay **to** the carry. Thus **the** long-unexplored main river, above the junction, came to be treated on the maps as a tributary, and to be dubbed the Wolf. This geographical mistake has been so long persisted in that correction becomes impracticable, and we must continue to style the branch the trunk.

This has been a delightful day; the heavens were clear and blue, and a gentle northeaster fanned our faces in the pilot-house, from which vantage-point, nearly thirty feet above the river-level, there was obtainable a bird's-eye view well worthy of canvas. The wild-rice bog, through which the Fox, here not over thirty yards wide, twists like the snapper of a whip, is from ten to fifteen miles wide, — a sea of living green, across which the breeze sends a regular succession of waves, losing themselves upon the far-distant shores. Upon the northwestern horizon, the Wolf comes stealing down at the base of a range of wooded hills. To the west, a flashing line tells where Lake Poygan " holds her mirror **to the sun.**" The tall smoke-stacks of the Winneconne saw-mills occupy the middle ground westward. To the east, in the centre of the picture, one catches glimpses of the consolidated stream, as its goodly flood quickly glides southeasterly, on a short spurt toward the Grand Butte des Morts, at the head of which is the old fur-trading village of the same name. Far southeastward, below the lake, there is just discernible the great brick chimney of a mammoth planing-mill, — an Algoma landmark, — and just behind that the black cloud resting above the Oshkosh factories. It is a broad, bounteous sweep of level landscape, — monotonous, of course, but imposing from mere immensity.

At the union of the rivers we bade farewell to our friend the captain; and the Doctor secured a promise from the engineer to send in his photograph to the hospital with which the former is connected. The "Ellen Hardy" stopped her engine as we cast off. In another minute, the great stern-wheel began to splash again, and we were bobbing up and down on the bubbly swell, waving farewell to our fellow-travelers and turning our prow to the southeast, while the roving "Ellen" shaped her course to Winneconne, where a lot of laths, destined for Princeton, awaited her arrival.

The low ridge which forms the eastern bank of the Wolf, down to the junction, soon slopes off to the northeast, in the direction of Appleton, leaving a broad, level plain, of great fertility, between it and Lakes Grand Butte des Morts and Winnebago. On this plain are built the cities of Oshkosh, Neenah, and Menasha. Across it, the northeaster, freshening to a lively breeze, had full sweep, and stirred up the Grand Butte des Morts into a wild display of opposition to our progress. Serried ranks of white-caps came sweeping across the lake, beating on our port bow, and the little sail, almost bursting with fulness, careened the canoe to the gunwale, as it swept gayly along through the foam. The paddles were necessary to keep her well abreast of the tide, and there was exercise enough in the operation to prevent drowsiness. The spray flew like a drizzling summer shower, but our baggage and stores were well covered down, and the weather was too warm for a body dampener to be uncomfortable.

We passed the dark, gloomy, tumbled-down, but picturesque village of Butte des Morts, just before entering the lake. Of the twenty-five or so houses in the place, all but two or three are guiltless of paint. There is a quaintness about the simple architecture, which gives Butte des Morts a distinctive appearance. To the initiated, it betokens the remains of an old fur-trading post ; and this was the genesis of Butte des Morts. It was in 1818 that Augustin Grignon and James Porlier, men intimately connected with the history of the French-Indian fur-trade in Wisconsin, set up their shanty dwellings and warehouses on a little lakeside knoll a mile below the present village, which was founded by their *voyageurs* on the site of an old Menomonee town and cemetery. Some of these post-buildings, together with the remains of the watch-tower, from which the traders obtained long advance notice of the approach of travelers, red or white, are still standing. As we sped by, I pointed out to the Doctor the location of these venerable relics, which I had, with proper enthusiasm, carefully inspected fully a dozen summers before, and he suggested that the knowledge of the approach of a possible customer, by means of the tower, gave the traders an excellent opportunity to mark up the goods.

James Porlier's son and successor, Louis B. Porlier, now an aged man, is the present occupant of the establishment, which is one of the oldest landmarks in Wisconsin ; and there, also, died the famous Augustin Grignon, historian of his clan. Butte des Morts, in the early day of the northwest, was something more than a trading-post. Situated near the union of the upper Fox and the Wolf, it was the rallying-point for both valleys, — long before Appleton, Neenah, Menasha or Oshkosh were known, or any of the towns on the upper Fox. It was the only white man's stopping-place between the portage and Kaukauna. The mail trail between Green Bay and the portage crossed here, — for strange to say, the great south-stretching widespread, which lies like a map before the village, was in those days firm enough for a horse to traverse with safety ; while to-day a boat can be pushed anywhere between the rushes and rice, and it is *par excellence* the great breeding-ground of this section for muskrats and water-fowl. A scow-ferry was maintained in pioneer times for the benefit of the mail-carrier and other travelers. Butte des Morts is mentioned in most of the journals left us by travelers over the Fox-Wisconsin watercourse, previous to 1835, and here several important Indian treaties were consummated by government commissioners.

It is somewhat over fifteen miles from the **mouth** of the Wolf to Oshkosh. The run down the lake seemed unusually protracted, for the city was clearly in sight the entire way, and the distance, over the flat expanse, was deceptive. Algoma, now a portion of Oshkosh, was something of a settlement long before the lower town began to grow. But the latter finally overtook and swallowed the original hamlet. Algoma is now chiefly devoted to the homes of the employees in the great planing and saw-milling establishments of Philetus Sawyer, Wisconsin's senior United States senator, and the wealthy Paine Brothers. The residences of these lumber kings are on a slope to the north of the iron wagon-bridge, under which we swept as the booming whistles of the busy locality, in unison with a noisy chorus of steam-gongs farther down the river, sounded the hour of six. Through the gantlet of the mills, with their outlying rafts, their lines of piling, and their great yards of newly sawn lumber, we sped quickly on. A half-hour later, we were turning up into a peaceful little dock alongside the south approach to the St. Paul railway-bridge, the canoe's quarters for the night. The sun was just plunging below the clear-cut prairie horizon, as we walked across the fields to the home of our expectant friends.

FOURTH LETTER.

THE LAND OF THE WINNEBAGOES.

APPLETON, WIS., June 10, 1887.

MY DEAR W——: We had a late start to-day from Oshkosh. It was half-past nine o'clock by the time we had reloaded our traps, pushed off from the railway embankment, and received the God-speed of M——, who had come down to see us off. The busy town, with its twenty-two thousand thrifty people, was all astir. The factories and the mills were resonant with the clang and rattle of industry, and across the two wagon-bridges of the city proper there were continual streams of traffic.

I suppose that Oshkosh is, in its way, as widely known throughout this country as almost any city in it. The name is strikingly outlandish, being equaled only by Kalamazoo, and furnishes the butt of many a newspaper joke and comic rhyme. Old chief Oshkosh, whose cognomen signifies "brave" in Menomonee speech, was the head man of his dusky tribe, a half-century ago. He was a doughty, wrinkled hero, o'er fond of fire-water, and wore a battered silk hat for a crown. About 1840, when the settlement here was four years old, the Government offered to establish a post-office if the inhabitants would unite on a name for the place. The whites favored Athens, but the Indians, half-breeds, and traders round about Butte des Morts, wanted their friend Oshkosh immortalized, so they came down to the new settlement in force, and the election being a free-for-all, carried the day. It is said that the Grignons were so anxious in behalf of the Menomonee sachem that they had a number of squaws array themselves in trousers and cast ballots like the bucks. And it was fortunate, as events proved, that the election turned out as it did, for the oddity of the name has been a permanent advertisement for a very bright community. Oshkosh, as hackneyed "Athens," would have been lost to fame. Nobody would think of going to "Athens" to "have fun with the boys."

The morning air was as clear as a bell, — a pleasant northeast zephyr, coming in off the body of the lake, slightly ruffling the surface and reducing the temperature to a delightful tone. The wind not being fair, the sail was useless, so we paddled along through the broad river, into the lake and northward past a fishermen's colony, **rows** of great **ice-houses, the** water-works park, and beautiful lake-shore residences, to Garlic Island. **It was half**-past twelve, P. M., when we tied up at the crazy pier which projects from this islet of the loud-smelling vegetable. A half-century ago Garlic Island was the home of Iowatuk, the beautiful aboriginal relict of a French fur-trader,—an Indian princess, the old settlers called her; at all events, she is reputed to have been a most exemplary person, well-possessed of this world's goods, as well **as a** large family of half-breed children. **The** island is charmingly situated, **a** half-mile **or more out** from the main land, opposite **the** Northern Insane Hospital; it is a forest **of** ancient elms, surrounded by a bowlder-strewn beach of some three quarters of a mile in length, and occupied by a summer-h**otel es**tablishment. The name "Garlic Island" **does** not sound very well for a fashionable resort, **so** the insular territory **has** been dubbed "Island Park" of late; but "Garlic" has good staying qualities, and I doubt if they can ever **efface** the objectionable pioneer title.

We had our dinner on the sward near the pier, convenient to a pump, and were entertained by watching the approach of a little steam-launch, loaded with a party of "resorters" who had doubtless been shopping in Oshkosh, the smoke from whose chimneys rose above the tree-tops, five miles to the southwest. There were some of the usual types,—the languid Southern woman, with her two pouting boys in charge of a rather savage-looking colored nurse, who dragged the little fellows out over the gang-plank, one in each hand, as though they had been bags of flour; a fashionable dame, from some northern metropolis, all ribbons and furbelows, starch and whalebones, accompanied by her willowy daughter of twenty, almost her counterpart as to dress, with a pert young miss of fourteen, in abbreviated gown and overgrown hat, bringing up the rear with the family pug; a dawdling young Anglo-maniac sucked the handle of his cane and looked sweetly on the society girl, whose papa, apparently a tired-out broker, in a well made business costume and a wretched straw hat, stayed behind to treat the skipper to a prime cigar and arrange for a fishing excursion.

There is a fine view from the island. The hills and cliffs of Calumet County, a dozen miles to the east, are dimly visible. Toward Fond du Lac, on the south, the horizon is the lake. South-southwestward, Black Wolf Point runs out, just over the verge, and the tops of the tall trees upon it peep up into view, like shadowy pile-work. Westward are the well-kept hospital grounds, fringed with stately elms overhanging the firm, gravelly beach, studded with ice-heaved bowlders, which extends northward to Neenah. The view to the north and northeast is delightfully hazy, being now dark with delicate fringes of forest which cap the occasional limestone promontories, and again losing itself in a watery sky-line.

We had two pleasant hours at this island-home of the lovely Iowatuk, walking around it on the bowldered beach, and reveling in the shade of the grand old elms. By the time we were ready to resume our voyage, the wind had died down, the lake was as smooth as a marble slab, and the sun's rays reflected from it converted the atmosphere to the temperature of a bake-oven. No sooner had we pushed out beyond the deep shadows of the trees than it seemed as though we had at one paddle-stroke shot into the waters of a tropic sea. The awning was at once raised, and served to somewhat mitigate our sufferings, but the **dazzling** reflection was there still, to **the** great discomfort of our eyes.

After two miles of distress, a bank of light but sharply broken clouds appeared on the northeastern horizon, and soon a gentle breeze brought blessed relief. In a few minutes more, ripples danced upon our starboard quarter, and then the awning had to come down, for it filled like a fixed sail and counteracted the effect of the paddles. The Doctor, who, you know full well, never paddles when he can sail, insisted on running up into the wind and spreading the canvas. He was just in time, for a squall struck us as he was adjusting the boom sprit, and nearly **sent** him overboard while attempting to regain his seat. Little black squalls now rapidly succeeded each other, the wind freshening between the gusts; and the Doctor, who was the sailing-master, had to exercise rare vigilance, for **the** breeze was rapidly developing into a young gale, and the ripples had now grown **to be** by far the largest waves our little **craft had yet** encountered. The situation began to be somewhat serious, as the clouds thickened and the white-caps broke upon the west beach with a sullen roar. We therefore deemed it advisable to run into a little harbor to the lee of a wooded spit, and hold council.

It was a wild, storm-tossed headland, two thirds of the distance down from the island, and the spit was but one of its many points. We landed and made an extended exploration, deeming **it possible that** we might be obliged to pass the night here; but the **result** of our discoveries was to discourage any such project. For a half-mile back or more the forest proved to be a tangled swamp, filled with fallen timber and sink-holes, while quicksands lined the harbor where the canoe peacefully rested behind an outlying fringe of gnarled elms. We wandered up and down the gravelly beach, in the spray of the breakers, scrambling over great bowlders and overhanging trunks whose foundations had been sapped by storm-driven floods; but everywhere was the same hard, forbidding scene of desolation, with the angry surface of the lake and the canopy of wind-clouds filling out a picture which, the Doctor suggested, could have only been satisfactorily executed in water-colors.

In the course of our wanderings, which were sadly destructive to clothes and shoe-leather, we had some comical adventures. The Doctor hasn't got over laughing about one of them yet. We came to an apparently shallow lagoon, perhaps three rods wide and a dozen long, beyond which we desired to penetrate. It was bedded with sand and covered with green slime. The Doctor had, just before, divested himself of shoes and stockings and rolled his trousers above his knees, in an enthusiastic hunt for a particularly ponderous frog, which he desired to pickle in the cause of science. He playfully offered to carry me across the pool on his back, and thus save me the trouble of imitating his style of undress. With some misgivings as to the result, I finally mounted. We progressed favorably as far as the centre, when suddenly I felt my transport sinking; he gave a desperate lunge as the water suddenly reached his waist, I sprang forward over his head, and losing my balance, sprawled out flat upon the slimy water. I hardly know how we reached firm ground again, but when we did, we were a sorry-looking pair, as you can well imagine. The Doctor thought it high sport, as he wrung out his clothes and spread them upon a bowlder to dry, and I tried hard to join in his boisterous hilarity; but somehow, as I scraped the gluey slime from my only canoeing suit, with a bit of old drift shingle, and contemplated the soppy condition of my wardrobe, I know there must have been a tinge of sadness in my gaze. It was too much like being shipwrecked on a desert island.

As we sat, clad in rubber coats, sunning ourselves on the lee side of a fallen tree and waiting for our garments to again become wearable, the Doctor read to me an article from his medical journal, describing a novel surgical operation on somebody's splintered backbone, copiously illustrating the selection with vivid reports of his own hospital observations in that direction. This sort of thing was well calculated to send the shivers down one's spinal column, but the Doctor certainly made the theme quite interesting and the half-hour necessary to the drying process soon passed.

By this time it was plain to be seen that the velocity of the wind was not going to increase before sundown, although it had not slacked. We determined to try the sea again, and pushed out through the breakers, with sail close-hauled and baggage canvased. Taking a bold offing into the teeth of the gale, we ran out well into the lower lake, and then, on a port tack, had a fine run down to Doty's Island, which divides the lower Fox into two channels. The city of Neenah, noted for its flouring and paper mills, is built upon both sides of the southern channel, or Neenah River; Menasha, with several factories, but apparently less prosperous than the other, guards the north channel,—the twin cities dividing the island between them. The government lock is at Menasha, while at Neenah there is a fine water-power, with a fall of twelve or fifteen feet,—the "Winnebago Rapids" of olden time.

It was into Neenah channel that we came flying so gayly, before the wind. There is a fine park on the mainland shore, with a smartly painted summer hotel and half a dozen pretty cottages that would do credit to a seaside resort. To the right the island is studded with picturesque old elms, shading a closely cropped turf, upon which cattle peacefully graze, while here and there among the trees are old-fashioned white cottages, with green blinds, quite after the style of a sleepy New-England village,—a charming scene of semi-rustic life; while to seaward Lake Winnebago tosses and rolls, almost to the horizon.

Doty's is an historic landmark. The rapids here necessitated a portage, and from the earliest times there have been Indian villages on the island, more or less permanent in character,—Menomonee, Fox, and Winnebago in turn. As white traffic over the Fox-Wisconsin watercourse grew, so grew the importance of this village, whatever the tribe of its inhabitants; for the bucks found employment in helping the empty boats over the rapids and in "toting" the goods over the portage-trail. The Foxes overreached themselves by setting up as toll-gatherers. It is related — but historians are somewhat misty as to the details — that in the winter of 1706-7 a French captain, Marin by name, was sent out by the governor of New France to chastise the blackmailers. At the head of a large party of French creoles and half-breeds, he ascended the lower Fox on snowshoes, surprising the aborigines in their principal village, here at Winnebago Rapids, and slaughtering them by the hundreds. Afterward, this same Marin conducted a summer expedition against the Foxes. His boats were filled with armed men and covered down with oilcloth, as traders were wont to treat their goods *en voyage*, to escape a wetting. Only two men were visible in each boat, paddling and steering. Nearly fifteen hundred dusky tax-gatherers were discovered squatting on the beach at the foot of the rapids, awaiting the arrival of the flotilla. The canoes were ranged along the shore. Upon a signal being given, the coverings were thrown off and volley after volley of hot lead poured into the mob of unsuspecting savages, a swivel-gun in Marin's boat aiding in the slaughter.

Tradition has it that over a thousand Foxes fell in that brutal assault. In 1716 another captain of New France, named De Louvigny, is reported to have stormed the audacious Foxes. They had not, it seems, been exterminated by previous massacres, for five hundred warriors and three thousand squaws are alleged to have been collected within a palisaded fort, somewhere in the neighborhood of these rapids. De Louvigny is credited with having captured the fort after a three days' siege, but granted the enemy the honors of war. Twelve years later the Foxes had again become so troublesome as to need chastisement. This time the agent chosen to command the expedition was De Lignery, among whose lieutenants was the noted Charles de Langlade, Wisconsin's first white settler. But the redskins had become wise, after their fashion, and fled before the Frenchmen, who found the villages on the Fox, lower and upper, deserted. The invaders burned every wigwam and cornfield in sight, from Green Bay to the portage. This expedition appears to have been followed by others, until the Foxes, with the allied Sacs, fled the valley, never to return. Much of this is traditionary.

The widening of the Fox below Doty's

Island was called **Lac** Petit Butte des Morts, —" Lake Little **Hill of** the Dead," to distinguish it from the **"Great** Hill **of** the Dead," above Oshkosh.

It has long been claimed **that** the thousands of **Foxes** who at various **times fell victims to** these massacres in behalf of **the French** fur-trade were buried in great pits at Petit **Butte des** Morts, — near Winnebago Rapids. But modern investigators lean to the opinion that the "little hill of **the** dead" was merely an ordinary Indian cemetery, and the mound **or** mounds there are prehistoric tumuli, common enough in the neighborhood of Wisconsin lakes. A like conclusion, **also,** has been arrived at in regard to the Grand Butte des Morts. However, this is something **that the** archæological committee must settle among **themselves.**

The Winnebagoes succeeded the Foxes, and Doty's Island became the seat of their power. The master spirit among them for a quarter of a century previous to the fall of New France was a French fur-trader named De Korra or **De Cora,** who had a Winnebago "princess" for a squaw. They had a numerous progeny, which **De Korra** left to his wife's charge **when called to** serve under Montcalm in the **defence of** Quebec. He was killed **in**

a sortie, and Madame De Korra and her brood relapsed into barbarism. One half of the Winnebagoes now living are descendants, more or less direct, of this sturdy old fur-trader, and bear his name, which is also perpetuated, with varied orthography, in many a northwestern stream and hamlet. During the first third of the present century Hoo-Tschope, or Four Legs, was the dusky magnate at this Winnebago capital.[1] Four Legs was a cunning rascal, well known to the earliest pioneers, but he at last fell a victim to his greatest enemy, the bottle. Last month I was visiting among the Winnebagoes around Black River Falls. Desiring to have a "talk" with Walking Cloud, a wizened-faced redskin of some seventy-two years, I went out with my interpreters over the hills and through the valley of the Black, nearly a dozen miles, before I found him and his squatting in their wigwams at the base of a bold bluff, fronted by a lovely bit of vale. Cloud's decrepit squaw, blind in one eye and wofully garrulous, hobbled up to us, and sinking to her knees in front of me, held out a dirty, bony hand, with nails like the claws of a bird, murmuring, "Give! Give!" I

---

[1] See Mrs. Kinzie's "Wau-Bun" for reminiscences of Four Legs.

dropped a coin into the outstretched palm; she grinned and chattered like an animated skeleton, and crawled away on her witch-like crutch. This was the once far-famed and beautiful princess of the **Winnebagoes,** the winsome Champche Keriwinke, or Flash of Lightning, eldest daughter of Hoo-Tschope. How are the mighty fallen!

We portaged around the island end of the Neenah dam and met the customary shallows below the obstruction. But soon finding a narrow, rock-imbedded channel, we glided swiftly down the stream, through the thrifty town, past the mills and under the bridges, just as the six o' clock bells had sounded and the factory hands were thronging homeward, their tin dinner-pails glistening in the sun. Scores of them stopped to lean over the bridge-rails, and curiously watched us as we threaded the shallows; for canoes long ago ceased to be a daily spectacle at Winnebago Rapids.

Little Lake Butte des Morts, just below, is where the river spreads to a full mile in breadth, the average width of the stream being less than one half that. The wind was fair, and we came swooping down into the lake, which is two or three miles long. A half-hour before sunset we hauled up at a high mossy glade on the north shore, and had delightful down-stream glimpses of deep vine-clad, naturally terraced banks, the slopes and summits being generally well wooded. A party of young men and women were having a camp near us. The woods echoed with their laughing shouts. A number, with their chaperone, a lovely and lively old lady, in a white cap with satin ribbons, came down to the shore to inspect our little vessel and question us as to our unusual voyage. We returned the call and played lawn tennis with fair partners, until the fact that we must reach Appleton to-night suddenly dawned upon us, and we bade a hasty farewell to our joyous wayside friends.

It was a charming run down to Appleton, between the park-like banks, which rise to an altitude of fifty feet or more. Every now and then a pretty summer residence stands prominently out upon a bluff-head, an architectural gem in a setting of oaks and luxurious pines. At their bases flows the deep flood of the Lower Fox, black as Erebus in the shadows, but smiling brightly in the patchy sunlight, and thickly decked with great bubbles which fairly leap along the course, eager to reach their far-off ocean goal. But swifter by far than the bubbles went our canoe as we set the paddles deeply and bent to our work, for the waters were strange to us, the night was setting in, and Appleton must be made. It will not do to traverse these rivers after dark unless well acquainted with the currents, the snags, and the dams, for disaster may readily overtake the unwary.

Cautiously we now crept along, for in the fast-fading twilight we could just discern the outlines of the Appleton paper-mills and a labyrinth of railway bridges, while the air fairly trembled with the mingled roar of water and of mighty gearing. Across the rapid stream shot piercing rays from the windows of the electric works, whose dynamos furnish light for the town and power for the street railway. A fisherman, tugging against the current, shouted to us to keep hard on the eastern bank, and in a few minutes more we glided by the stone pier which buttresses the upper dam, and pulled up in a little dead-water cove at the base of the Milwaukee and Northern railway bridge. The bridge-tender's children came down to meet us; the man himself soon followed; we were permitted to chain up for the night at his pier, and to deposit our bulky baggage in his kitchen; he accompanied us over the long bridge which spans the noisy apron and the rushing race. A misstep between the ties would send one on a short cut to the hereafter, but we safely crossed, ascended two or three steep flights of stairs to the top of the bank, and in a minute or two more were speeding up town to our hotel, aboard an electric street railway car.

FIFTH LETTER.

LOCKED THROUGH.

LITTLE KAUKAUNA, WIS., June 11, 1887.

MY DEAR W——: We took an extended stroll around Appleton after breakfast. It is a beautiful city,—the gem of the Lower Fox. The banks are nearly one hundred feet high above the river level. They are deeply cut with ravines. Hillside torrents, quickly formed by heavy rains, as quickly empty into the stream, draining the plateau of its superfluous surface water, and in the operation carving these great gulches through the soft clay. And so there are many steep inclines in the Appleton highways, and the ravines are frequently bridged by dizzy trestle-works; but the greater part of the city is on a high, level plain, the wealthy dwellers courting the summits of the river banks, where the valley view is panoramic. The little Methodist college, with its high-sounding title of Lawrence University, is an excellent institution, and said to be growing; it gives a certain scholastic tinge to Appleton society, which might otherwise be given up to the worship of Mammon, for there is much wealth among the manufacturers who rule the city, and prosperity attends their reign.

There is a good natural water-power here, but the Fox-Wisconsin improvement has made it one of the finest in the world. If the improvement scheme is a flat failure elsewhere, as is beginning to be generally believed, it certainly has been the making of this valley of the Lower Fox. From Lake Winnebago down to the mouth, the rapids are frequent, the chief being at Neenah, Appleton, Kaukauna, Little Kaukauna, and Depere. Of the twenty-six locks from Portage down, seventeen are below our stopping-point of last night; the fall at each, at this stage of water being about twelve feet on the average. Each of these locks involves a dam; and when the stream is thus stemmed and all repairs maintained, at the expense of the general government, it is a simple matter to tap the reservoir, carry a race along the bank, and have water-power *ad libitum*. Not half the water-power in sight, not a tenth of that possible is used. There is enough here, experts declare, to turn the machinery of the world. No wonder the beautiful valley of the Lower Fox is rich, and growing richer.

It was no holiday excursion to portage around the Appleton locks this morning. At none of them could we find the tenders, for the Menasha lock being broken, there is no through navigation from Oshkosh to Green Bay this week, and way traffic is slight. We had neglected to furnish ourselves with a tin horn, and the vigorous use of lung power failed to achieve the desired result. The banks being steep and covered with rock chips left by the stone-cutters employed on the work, we had some awkward carries, and felt, as we finally passed the cordon and set out on the straight eastward stretch for Kaukauna, that we were earning our daily bread.

Kaukauna, the Grand Kackalin of the Jesuits and early French traders, is ten miles below Appleton. Here are the most formidable rapids on the river, the fall being sixty feet, down an irregular series of jagged limestone stairs some half mile in extent. Indians, in their light bark canoes and practically without baggage, can, in high water, make the passage, up or down, by closely hugging the deeper and stiller water on the north bank ; but the French traders invariably portaged their goods, allowing the voyageurs to carry over the empty boats, the men walking in the water by the side, pushing, hauling, and balancing, amid a stream of oaths from their bourgeois, or master, who remained at his post. I had had an idea that in our little craft we might safely make the venture of a shoot down the stairs, by exercising caution and following the Indian channel. But this was previous to arrival. Leaving the Doctor to guard the canoe from a crowd of Kaukauna urchins, who were disposed to be over-familiar with our property, I went down through a boggy field to view the situation. It is a grand sight, looking up from the bottom of the rapids. The water is low, and at every few rods masses of rock project above the seething flood, specimens of what line the channel. The torrent comes down with a mighty roar, lashing itself into a fury of spray and foam as it leaps around and over the obstructions, and takes great lunges from step to step. There are several curves in the basin of the cataract, which add to its artistic effect, while it is deeply fringed by stunted pines and scrub oaks, having but a slender footing in the shallow turf which covers the underlying stratum of limestone. Whatever may be the condition of the falls at Kaukauna in high water, it is certain that at this stage a canoe would be dashed to splinters quite early in the attempt to scale them.

But a portage of half a mile was not to our taste in the torrid temperature we have been experiencing to-day, and we determined to maintain the rights of free navigators by obliging the tenders to put us through the five great locks, which are here necessary to lower vessels from the upper to the lower level. These tenders receive ample compensation, and many of them are notoriously lazy. It is but seldom that they are compelled to exercise their muscles on the gates; for navigation on the Fox is spasmodic and unimportant. As I have said in one of my previous letters, even a saw-log has the right of way; and government paid a goodly sum to the speculators from whom it purchased this improvement, that free tollage might be established here for all time. And so it was that, perhaps soured a little by our Appleton experience, we determined at last to test the matter and assert the privileges of American citizens on a national highway.

On regaining my messmate, we took a general view of Kaukauna, — which spreads over the banks and a prairie bottom on both sides of the river, and is a growing, bustling, freshly built little factory town, — and then re-embarked to try our fortune at the lock-gates. Heretofore we had considerately portaged every one of these obstructions, except at Princeton, where we went through under the "Ellen Hardy's" wing.

A stalwart Irishman, in his shirt-sleeves, and smoking a clay pipe with that air of dogged indifference peculiar to so many government officials, leaned over a capstan at the upper lock, and dreamily stared at the approaching canoe. The lock was full, the last boat having passed up a day or two before. The upper gates being open, we pushed in, and took up our station in the centre of the basin, to avoid the "suck" during the emptying process. The Doctor took out of the locker a copy of his medical journal and I a novel, and we settled down as though we had come to stay. The Irishman's face was at first a picture of dumb astonishment, and then he sullenly picked up his coat from the grass, and began to walk off in the direction of the town.

"Hi, my friend!" shouted the Doctor, good-naturedly. "We are waiting to get locked through."

The tender returned a step, his eyes opened wide, his brows knit, and in his wrath he stuttered, "Ph-h-a-t! Locked through in that theer s-s-k-i-ff? Ye're cr-razy, mon!"

"Oh, not at all. We understand our rights, and wish you to lock us through. And, if you please, we're in something of a hurry." As I said this I consulted my watch, and after returning it to my pocket resumed a vacant gaze upon the outspread leaves of the novel.

The tender — for we had guessed rightly; it was the tender — advanced to the edge of the basin, and looked with inexpressible scorn upon our Liliputian craft. "Now, look here, gints," he said, somewhat more conciliatory, "I've been here for twinty years, an' know the law; an' the law don't admit no skiffs, ye mind y'ur eye. An' the divil a bit of lockage will ye git here, an' mind that!" And then he walked away.

We were very patient. The rim of the lock became lined with small boys and smaller girls, for this is Saturday, and a school holiday; and there was great wonderment at the men in the canoe, who "were having a bloody old row with Barney, the lock-tinder," as one boy vigorously expressed the situation to a bevy of new-comers. By and by Barney returned to see if we were still there. We were, and were so abstracted that we did not heed his presence.

"Will, ye ain't gone yit, I see?" said Barney.

The Doctor roused himself, and pulling out his watch, appeared to be greatly surprised. "I do declare," he ejaculated, "if we have n't been waiting here nearly half an hour! I say, my man, this sort of delay is inexcusable. It will read badly in a report to the Engineering Bureau. What is your number, sir?" And with a stern expression he produced his tablets, prepared to jot down the numeral.

Barney was clearly weakening. His return to see if the "bluff" had worked was an evidence of that. The Doctor's severe official manner, and our quiet persistence appeared to convince Barney that he had made a grave mistake. So he hurried off to the lower capstans, growling something about being "oft'n fooled with fish'n' parties." When we were through we left Barney a cigar on the curbing, and gently admonished him never again to be so rude to canoeists, or some day he would get reported. As we pushed off he bade us an affectionate farewell, and said he had sent his "lad" ahead to see that we had no trouble at the four lower locks. We did not see the lad; but certain it is that the other tenders were prompt and courteous, and we felt that the cigars which we distributed along the Kaukauna Canal were not illy bestowed.

Progress was slow to-day, owing to the delays in locking. Ordinarily, we make from thirty to forty miles, — on the Rock, you remember, we averaged forty. But it was nearly sunset when we passed under the old wagon bridge at Wrightstown, only seventeen miles below our starting-point of this morning. We paused for a minute or two, to talk with a peaceably disposed lad, who was the sole patron of the bridge and lay sprawled across the board foot-walk, with his head under the railing, fishing as contentedly as though he lay on a grassy bank, after the manner of the gentle Izaak. When old Mr. Wright was around, Wrightstown may have been quite a place. But it is now going the way of so many river towns. There is a small, rickety saw-mill in operation, to which farmers from the back country haul in pine logs, of which there are some hundreds neatly piled in an adjoining field. Another saw-mill shell is hard by, the home of owls and bats, — a deserted skeleton, whose spirit, in the shape of machinery, has departed to Ashland, a more modern paradise of the buzz-saw. The village, dressed in that tone of pearly gray with which kind Nature decks those habitations left paintless by neglectful man, — is prettily situated on the high banks which uniformly hedge in the Lower Fox. On the highest knoll of all is a modest little frame church whose spire — white, after a fashion — is a prominent landmark to river travelers. There are the remains of once well-kept gardens, upon the upper terraces; of somewhat elaborate fences, now swaying to and fro and weak in the knees; of sidewalks which have become pitfalls; of impenetrable thickets of lilacs, hedging lonely spots that once were homes. On the village street, only a few idlers were seen, gathered in knots of two or three in front of the barber shop and the saloons; the smith at his forge was working late, shoeing a country team; and two angular dames, in rusty sun-bonnets, were gossiping over a barnyard gate. That was all we saw of Wrightstown, as we drifted northward in company with the reeling bubbles, down through the deepening shadow cast by the western bank.

Here and there, where the land chances to slope gently to the water's edge, are small piles of logs, drawn on farm sleds during the winter season from depleted pineries, all the way from three to ten miles back. When wanted at the saw-mills down the river, or just above, at Wrightstown, they are loosely made up into small rafts and poled to market. Along the stream there are but few pines left, and they generally crown some rocky ledge, not easily accessible. A few small clumps are preserved, however, relics of the forest's former state, to adorn private grounds or enhance the gloomy tone of little hillside cemeteries. There must have been an impressive grandeur about the scenery of the Lower Fox in the early day, before the woodman's axe leveled the great pines which then swept down in solid rank to the river beach, closely hedging in the dark and rapid flood.

We lunched upon a stone terrace, above which swayed in the evening breeze the dense, solemn branches of a giant native, one of the last of his fated race. The channel curved below, and the range of vision was short, between the stately banks, heavily fringed as they are with aspen and scrub-oak. As we sat in the gathering gloom and gayly chatted over the simple adventures which are making up this week of ideal vacation life, there came up from the depths below the steady swish and pant of a river steamboat,— rare object upon our lonesome journey. As the bulky craft came slowly around the bend, the pant became a subdued roar, awakening a dull echo from the wooded slopes. A small knot of passengers lolled around the pilot-house, on which we were just able to discern the name "Evalyn, of Oshkosh," in burnished gilt; on the freight deck there were bales and boxes of merchandise, and heaps of lumber; two stokers were feeding cord-wood to the furnace flames, which lit the scene with lurid glare, after the fashion of theatric fires; the roustabouts were fastening night lanterns to the rails. The V-shaped wake of her wheel-barrow stern broke upon the shores like a tidal wave, and the canoe, luckily well fastened to the roots of a stranded tree, bobbed up and down as would a chip tossed on the billows.

Four miles below Wrightstown is Little Kaukauna. There are three or four cottages here, well up on the pleasant western bank, overlooking a deserted saw-mill property; while just beyond, a government lock does duty whenever needed, and the rest of the now broadened stream is stemmed by a magnificent dam, from the foot of which arises a dense cloud of vapor, such is the force of the torrent which pours with a mighty sweep over the great chute. As we stole down upon the hamlet, the moon, a day or two past full, was just rising over the opposite hillocks; a tall pine standing out boldly from its lesser fellows, was **weirdly** silhouetted across her beaming face, **and in** the cottage windows lights gleamed a homely welcome.

We were cordially received at the house **of** the patriarch of the settlement. **We made** our craft secure for the night, "toted" our baggage up the bank, **and paused upon the** broad porch **of our** new-found friend to contemplate a most charming moonlit view of river and forest and glade and cataract; the cloud of mist rising high **above** the roaring declivity seemed as an incense offering to the goddess of the night.

SIXTH LETTER.

THE BAY SETTLEMENT.

GREEN BAY, WIS., June 13, 1887.

MY DEAR W——: We had a quiet Sunday at Little Kaukauna. Being a delightful day, we went with our entertainers to the country church, a mile or two back across the fields, and whiled away the rest of the time in strolling through the woods and gossiping with the farmers about the crops and the government improvement, — fertile themes. It appears that this diminutive hamlet of four or five houses anticipates a "boom," and there is some feverish anxiety as to how much village lots ought to bring as a "starter" when the rush actually opens. A syndicate has purchased the long-abandoned water-power, and it is whispered that paper-mills are to be erected, with cottages for operatives, and all that sort of thing. Then, the church and the depot will have to be brought into town; the proprietor of the cross-roads grocery, now out on the "country road," will be erecting a brick "block" by the river side; somebody will be starting a daily paper, printed from stereotype plates imported from Oshkosh or Chicago; and a summer resort hotel with a magnetic spring, will doubtless cap the climax of village greatness. I shall look with interest on reports from the Little Kaukauna boom.

It was nine o'clock this morning before we dipped paddle and bore down to the lock gates. The good-natured tender "dropped" us through with much alacrity. The river gradually widens, and here and there the high rolling banks recede for some distance, and marshes and bayous, excellent hunting-grounds, border the stream. A half mile below the lock we noticed a roughly built hut, open at front, such as would quarter a pig in the shanty outskirts of a great city. It looked lonesome, on the edge of a wide bog, with no other sign of habitation, either human or animal, in the watery landscape. Curiosity impelled us to stop. Crossing a plank, which rested one end on a snag and the other on a stone in front of the three-sided structure, we peered in. A bundle of rags lay in one corner of the floor of loosely laid boards; in another was a heap of clamshells, the contents of which had doubtless been cooked over a little fire which still smouldered in a neighboring clump of reeds. The odors were noisome, and a foot rise of water would have swamped out the dweller in this strange abode. We at once took it for granted that this was either the home of an Indian or a tramp. Just as we were leaving, however, a frowsy, dirty, but apparently good-tempered fisherman came rowing up and claimed the cabin as his home. He said that he spent the greater part of the year in this filthy hole, hunting or fishing according to the season; in the winter, he boarded up the front, leaving a hole to crawl out of, and banked the hut about with reeds and muck. Wrightstown was his market; and he "managed to scratch," he said, by being economical. I asked him how much it cost him in cash to exist in this state, which was but slightly removed from the condition of our ancestral cave-dwellers. He thought that with twenty-five dollars in cash, he could "manage to scratch finely" for an entire year, and have besides "a week off with the boys," — in other words, one prolonged drinking bout, — at Wrightstown. He complained, however, that he seldom received money, being mainly put off with barter. The poor fellow, evidently something of a simpleton, is probably the victim of sharp practice occasionally. As we paddled away from this singular character, the Doctor said that he had a novel-writing friend, given to the sensational, to whom he would like to introduce The Wild Fisherman of Little Kaukauna; he thought there was material for a romance here, particularly if it could be proved, as was quite possible, that the hut man was the lost heir of a British dukedom.

But the site of another and a stranger romance is but half a mile farther down. The river there suddenly broadens into a basin, fully half a mile in width. To the east, the banks are quite abrupt. The westward shore is a gentle, grass-grown slope, stretching up beyond a charming little bay formed by a spit of meadow. Near the sandy beach of this bay a country highway passes, winding in and out and up and down, as it follows the river and the bases of the knolls. Above this and commanding delightful glimpses of forest and stream and bayou and prairie, a goodly hillock is crowned, some seventy-five feet above the water's edge, with a dark, unpainted, time-worn, moss-grown house, part log and part frame, set in a deep tangle of lilacs and crabs. The quaint old structure is of the simple pioneer pattern, — a story and a half, with gables on the north and south ends of the main part ; and a small transverse wing to the rear, with connecting rooms. The ancient picket gate creaks on its one rusty hinge. The front door has the appearance of being nailed up, and across its frame a dozen fat spiders, most successful of fly fishers, have stretched their gluey nets. The path, once leading thither, is now o'ergrown with grass and lilacs, while in the surrounding snarl of weeds and poplar suckers are seen the blossoming remnants of peonies, and a few old-fashioned garden shrubs.

The ground is historic. The house is an ancient landmark. It was the old home of Eleazar Williams, in his day Episcopal missionary and pretender to the throne of France. Williams was the reputed son of a mixed-blood couple of the Mohawk band of Indians; in early life, he claimed to have been born in the vicinity of Montreal, in 1792. A bright youth, he was educated for the ministry of the Protestant Episcopal church and sent as a missionary in 1816–1817 to the Oneida Indians, then located in Oneida county, New York. During the war of 1812, he had been employed as a spy by the American authorities to trace the movements of British troops in Canada. Williams, from the first, became engaged in intrigues among the New York Indians, and was the originator of the movement which resulted, in 1822, in the purchase by the war department of a large strip of land from the Menomonees and Winnebagoes, along the Lower Fox River, and the removal hither of several of the New York bands, accompanied by the scheming priest. But the result was jealousy between the newcomers and the original tribes, with sixteen years of confusion and turmoil, during which Congress was frequently engaged in settling the squabbles that arose. Williams's original idea was said, by those who knew him best, to be the "total subjugation of the whole [Green Bay] country and the establishment of an Indian government, of which he was to be sole dictator."[1]

But his purpose failed. He came to be recognized as an unscrupulous fellow, and the majority of the whites and Indians on the Lower Fox, as well as his clerical brethren, regarded him with contempt. In 1853, Williams, baffled in every other field of notoriety which he had worked, suddenly posed before the American public as Louis XVII., heredi-

[1] Wis. Hist. Colls., vol. ii. p. 425.

tary sovereign of France. Upon the downfall of the Bourbons in 1792, you will remember that Louis XVI. and his queen, Marie Antoinette, were beheaded, while their son, the dauphin Louis, an imbecile child of eight, was cast into the temple tower by the revolutionists. It is officially recorded that after an imprisonment of two years the dauphin died in the tower and was buried. But the story was started and popularly believed, that the real dauphin had been abducted by the royalists and another child cunningly substituted to die there in the dauphin's place. The story went that the dauphin had been sent to America and all traces of him lost, thus giving any adventurer of the requisite age and sufficiently obscure birth, opportunity to seek such honor as might be gained in claiming identity with the escaped prisoner. Williams was too young by eight years to be the dauphin; he was clearly of Indian extraction,—a fair type of the half-breed, in color, form, and feature. But he succeeded in deceiving a number of good people, including several leading doctors in his church; while an Episcopal clergyman named John H. Hanson attempted, in two articles in "Putnam's Magazine," in 1853, and afterwards in an elaborate book, "The Lost Prince," to prove conclusively to the world that Williams was indeed the son of the executed monarch. While those who really knew Williams treated his claims as fraudulent, and his dusky father and mother protested under oath that Eleazar was their son, and every allegation of Williams, in the premises, had been often exposed as false, there were still many who believed in him. The excitement attracted attention in France. One or two royalists came over to see Williams, but left disappointed; and Louis Philippe sent him a present of some finely bound books, believing him to be the innocent victim of a delusion. Williams died in 1858, keeping up his absurd pretensions to the last.

It was in this house near Little Kaukauna that Williams lived for so many years, managing and preaching to his scattered flock of immigrant Indians, and forever seeking some sort of especially profitable employment, such as accompanying tribal delegations to Washington, or acting as special commissioner at government payments. In the earliest days, the house was situated on the spit of meadow I have previously spoken of; but when the dam at Depere raised the water, the frame was carried to this higher position.

Williams's wife, an octoroon, whose portrait shows her to have been a thick-set, stolid sort of woman, died here, a year ago, and is buried hard by. The present occupants of the house are Mary Garritty, an Indian woman of sixty-five years, and her half-breed daughter, Josephine Penney, who in turn has an infant child of two. Mary was reared by the Williamses, and told us many a curious story of life at the "agency," as she called it, during the time when "Mr. Williams and Ma" were alive. Josephine, who confided to me that she was thirty years old, was regularly adopted by Mrs. Williams, for whose memory both women seem to have a very strong respect. What little personal property was left by the old woman goes to her grandchildren, intelligent and well-educated Oshkosh citizens, but Josephine has the sandy farm of sixty-five acres. She took me into the attic to exhibit such relics of the alleged dauphin as had not been disposed of by the administrator of the estate. There were a hundred or two mice-eaten volumes, mainly theological and school text-books; several old volumes of sermons, — for Eleazar is said to have considered it better taste in him to copy a discourse from an approved authority than to endeavor to compose one that would not satisfy him half as well; a boxful of manuscript odds and ends, chiefly letters, Indian glossaries and copied sermons; two or three leather-bound trunks, a copper tea-kettle used by him upon his long boat journeys, and a pair of antiquated brass candlesticks.

Then we descended to the old orchard. Mary pointed out the spot, a rod or two south of the dwelling, where Williams had his library and mission-office in a log-house that has long since been removed for firewood. In this cabin, which had floor dimensions of fifteen by twenty feet, Williams met his Indian friends and transacted business with them. Mary, in her querulous tone, said that in those days the place abounded with Indians, night and day, and as they always expected to be fed, she had her hands full attending to their wants. "There wa'n't no peace at all, sir, so long as Mr. Williams were here; when he were gone there wa'n't so many of them, an' we got a rest, which I were mighty thankful for." Garrulous Mary, in her moccasins and blanket skirt, with a complexion like brown parchment and as wrinkled, — almost a full-blood herself, — has lived so long apart from her people that she appears to have forgotten her race, and inveighed right vigorously against the unthrifty and beggarly habits of the aborigines. "I hate them pesky Indians," she cried in a burst of righteous indignation, and then turned to croon over Josephine's baby, as veritable a "little Indian boy" as I ever met with in a forest wigwam. "He's a fine feller, is n't he?" she cried, as she chucked her grandson under the chin; "some says as he looks like Mr. Williams, sir." The Doctor, who is a judge of babies, declared, in a professional tone that did not admit of contradiction, that the infant was, indeed, a fine specimen of humanity.

And thus we left the two women in a most contented frame of mind, and descended to the beach, bearing with us Josephine's parting salute, shouted from the garden gate,— "Call agin, whene'er ye pass this way!"

Depere is five miles below. The banks are bold as far as there; but beyond, they flatten out into gently sloping meadows, varied here and there by the re-approach of a high ridge on the eastern shore,— the western getting to be quite marshy by the time Fort Howard is reached.

At Depere are the first rapids of the Fox, the fall being about twelve feet. From the earliest period recorded by the French explorers, there was a polyglot Indian settlement upon the portage-trail, and in December, 1669, the Jesuit missionary Allouez established St. Francis Xavier mission here, the locality being henceforth styled " Rapide des **Peres." It was from** this station that Allouez, Dablon, Joliet, and Marquette started upon their memorable canoe voyages up the Fox, in search of benighted heathen and the Mississippi River. For over a century Rapide des Peres was a prominent landmark in Northwestern history. The Depere of to-day is a solid-looking town, with an iron furnace, sawmills, and other industries; and after a long period of stagnation is experiencing a healthy business revival.

Unable to find the tender at this the last lock on our course, we portaged after the manner **of** old-time canoeists, and set out upon the home stretch of six miles. Green Bay, upon **the** eastern bank and Fort Howard upon the **western,** were well in view; and, it being not past **two** o'clock in the afternoon of a cool and somewhat cloudy day, we allowed the current to be our chief propeller, only now and then using the paddles to keep our bark well in the main current.

The many pretty residences of South Green Bay, including the ruins of Navarino, Astor, **and** Shanty Town, are situated well up on an attractive sloping ridge; **but** the land soon **drops** to an almost swampy level, upon which the greater portion of the business quarter is built. Opposite, Fort Howard with her mills and coal-docks skirts a wide-spreading bog, much of the flat, sleepy old town being built on a foundation of saw-mill offal. Historically, both sides of the river may be practically treated as the old " Bay Settlement," for two and a half centuries one of the most conspicuous outposts of American civilization. Here came savage-trained Nicolet, exploring agent of Champlain, in 1634, when Plymouth colony was still in swaddling-clothes. It was the day when the China Sea was supposed to be somewhere in the neighborhood of the Great Lakes. Nicolet had heard that at Green Bay he would meet a strange people, who had come from beyond " a great water " to the west. He was therefore prepared to meet here a colony of Chinamen or Japanese, if indeed Green Bay were not the Orient itself. His mistake was a natural one. The "strange people" were Winnebago Indians. A branch of the Dakotahs, or Sioux, a distinct race from the Algonquins, they forced themselves across the Mississippi River, up the Wisconsin, and down the Fox, to Green Bay, entering the Algonquin territory like a wedge, and forever after maintaining their foothold upon this interlocked water highway. "The great water,"

The Bay Settlement. 231

supposed by Nicolet to mean the China Sea, was the Mississippi River, beyond which barrier the Dakotah race held full sway. As he approached, one of his Huron guides was sent forward to herald his coming. Landing near the mouth of the river, he attired himself in a gorgeous damask gown, decorated with gayly colored birds and flowers, expecting to meet mandarins who would be similarly dressed. A horde of four or five thousand naked savages greeted him. He advanced, discharging the pistols which he held in either hand, and women and children fled in terror from the manitou who carried with him lightning and thunder.

The mouth of the Fox was always a favorite rallying-point for the savages of this section of the Northwest, and many a notable council has been held here between tribes of painted red men and Jesuits, traders, explorers, and military officers. Being the gateway of one of the two great routes to the Mississippi, many notable exploring and military expeditions have rested here; and French, English, and Americans in turn have maintained forts to protect the interests of territorial possession and the fur-trade.

Here it was that a white man first set foot on Wisconsin soil; and here, also, in 1745, the De Langlades, first permanent settlers of the Badger State, reared their log cabins and initiated a semblance of white man's civilization. Green Bay, now hoary with age, has had an eventful, though not stirring history. For a hundred years she was a distributing-point for the fur-trade.

The descendants of the De Langlades, the Grignons and other colonists of nearly a century and a half standing, are still on the spot; and the gossip of the hour among the *voyageurs* and old traders still left among us is of John Jacob Astor, Ramsay Crooks, Robert Stuart, Major Twiggs, and other characters of the early years of our century, whose names are well known to frontier history. The creole quarter of this ancient town, shiftless and improvident to-day as it always has been, lives in an atmosphere hazy with poetic glamour, reveling in the recollection of a once festive, half-savage life, when the *courier de bois* and the *engagé* were in the ascendency at this forest outpost, and the fur-trade the be-all and end-all of commercial enterprise. Your *voyageur*, scratching a painful living for a hybrid brood from his meager potato patch, bemoans the day when Yankee progressiveness dammed the Fox for Yankee saw-mills, into whose insatiable maws were swept the forests of his youth, and remembers nought but the sweets of his early calling among his boon companions, the denizens of the wilderness.

In Shanty Town, Astor, and Navarino there yet remain many dwellings and trading warehouses of the olden time, — unpainted, gaunt, poverty-stricken, but with their hand-hewed skeletons of oak still intact beneath the rags of a century's decay. A hundred years is a period quite long enough in our land to warrant the brand of antiquity, although a mere nothing in the prolonged career of the Old World. In the rapidly developing West, a hundred years and less mark the gap between a primeval wilderness and a complete civilization. Time, like space, is, after all, but comparative. In these hundred years the Northwest has developed from nothing to everything. It is as great a period, judging by results, as ten centuries in Europe, — perhaps fifteen. America is said to have no history. On the contrary, it has the most romantic of histories; but it has lived faster and crowded more and greater deeds into the past hundred years than slow-going Europe in the last ten hundred. The American centenarian of to-day is older by far than the fabled Methuselah.

Green Bay, classic in her shanty ruins, has

been somewhat halting in her advance, for the creoles hamper progressiveness. But as the *voyageurs* and their immediate progeny gradually pass away, the community creeps out from the shadow of the past and asserts itself. The ancient town appears to be taking on a new and healthy growth, in strange contrast to the severe and battered architecture of frontier times. Socially, Green Bay is delightful. There are many old families, whose founders were engaged in superintending the fur-trade and transportation lines, or holding government office, civil or military, at the wilderness post. This element, well educated and reared in comfort, gives a tone of dignified, old-school hospitality to the best society,—it is the Knickerbocker Colony of the Bay Settlement.

At four o'clock we pushed into a canal in front of the Fort Howard railway depot, and half an hour later had crossed the bridge and were registered at a Green Bay hotel. The Doctor, called home to resume the humdrum of his hospital life, will leave for the South to-morrow noon. I shall remain here for a week, reposing in the shades of antiquity.

THE WISCONSIN RIVER.

THE WISCONSIN RIVER.

CHAPTER I.

ALONE IN THE WILDERNESS.

OUR watches, for a wonder, coincided on Monday afternoon, Aug. 22, 1887. This phenomenon is so rare that W—— made a note in her diary to the effect that for once in its long career my time-piece was right. It was five minutes past two. The place was the beach at Portage, just below the old red wagon-bridge which here spans the gloomy Wisconsin. A teamster had hauled us, our canoe, and our baggage from the depot to the verge of a sand-bank; and we had dragged our faithful craft down through a tangle of sand-burrs and tin cans to the water's edge, and packed the locker for its third and final voyage of the season. A

German housewife, with red kerchief, cap, and tucked-up skirt, stood out in the water on the edge of a gravel-spit, engaged in her weekly wrestle with the family wash,—a picturesque, foreign-looking scene. On the summit of a sandy promontory to our left, two other German housewives leaned over a pig-yard fence and gazed intently down at these strange preparations. Back of us were the wooded sand-drifts of Portage, once a famous camping-ground of the Winnebagoes; before us, the dark, treacherous river, with its shallows and its mysterious depths; beyond that, great stretches of sand-fields thick-strewn with willow forests and, three or four miles away, the forbidding range of the Baraboo Bluffs, veiled in the heavy mist which was rapidly closing upon the valley.

We feared that we were booked for a stormy trip, as we pushed out into the bubble-strewn current and found that a cold east wind was blowing over the flats and rowing-jackets were essential.

Portage City, a town of twenty-five hundred inhabitants, occupies the southeastern bank for a mile down. Like Green Bay and Prairie du Chien, it was an outgrowth of the necessities of the early fur-trade. Upon the death of that trade it languished and for a generation or two was utterly stagnant. As a rural trading centre it has since grown into a state of fair prosperity, although the presence of many of the old-time buildings of the Indian traders and transporters gives to much of the town a sadly decayed appearance. For two or three miles we had Portage in view, down a straight course, until at last the thickening mist hid the time-worn houses from view, and we were fairly on our way down the historic Wisconsin, in the wake of Joliet and Marquette, who first traversed this highway to the Mississippi, two hundred and fourteen years ago.

Marquette, in the journal of his memorable voyage, says of the Wisconsin, "It is very broad, with a sandy bottom, forming many shallows, which render navigation very difficult." The river has been frequently described in the journals of later voyagers, and government engineers have written long reports upon its condition, but they have not bettered Marquette's comprehensive phrase.

The general government has spent enormous sums in an endeavor to make the Fox-Wisconsin water highway practicable for the passage of large steam-vessels between the Great Lakes and the Mississippi River. It was of great service, in its natural state, for the passage into the heart of the continent of that motley procession of priests, explorers, cavaliers, soldiers, trappers, and traders who paddled their canoes through here for nearly two hundred years, the pioneers of French, English, and American civilization in turn. It is still a tempting scheme, to tap the main artery of America, and allow modern vessels of burden to make the circuit between the lakes and the gulf. The Fox River is reasonably tractable, although this season the stage of water above Berlin has been hardly high enough to float a flat-boat. But the Wisconsin remains, despite the hundreds of wing-dams which line her shores, a fickle jade upon whom no reliance whatever can be placed. The current and the sand-banks shift about at their sweet will over a broad valley, and the pilot of one season would scarcely recognize the stream another. Navigation for crafts drawing over a foot of water is practically impossible in seasons of drought, and uncertain in all. A noted engineer has playfully said that the Wisconsin can never be regulated, " until the bottom is lathed and plastered ;" and another officially reported, over fifteen years ago, that nothing short of a continuous canal along the bank, from Portage to Prairie du Chien, will suffice to meet the expectations of those who favor the government improvement of this impossible highway.

In the neighborhood of Portage, the wing-dams, — composed of mattresses of willow boughs, weighted with stone, — are in a reasonable degree of preservation and in places appear to be of some avail in contracting the channel. But elsewhere down the river, they are generally mere hindrances to canoeing. The current, as it caroms from shore to shore, pays but little heed to these obstructions and we often found it swiftest over the places where black lines of willow twigs bob and sway above the surface of the rushing water; while the channel staked out by the engineers was the site of a sand-field, studded with aspen-brush.

It is a lonely run of an hour and a half down to the mouth of the Baraboo River, through the mazes of the wing-dams, surrounded by desolate bottom lands of sand and wooded bog. The east wind had brought a smart shower by the time we had arrived off the mouth of this northern tributary and we hauled up at a low, forested bank just below the junction, where rubber coats were brought out and canvas spread over the stores. The rain soon settled into a mere drizzle, and W——, ever eager in her botanical researches, wandered about regardless of wet feet, investigating the flora of the locality. The yellow sneeze-weed and purple iron-weed predominate in great clumps upon the verge of the bank, and lend a cheerful tone to what would otherwise be a desolate landscape.

The drizzle finally ceasing, we were again afloat, and after shooting by scores of wing-dams that had been "snowed under" by shifting sand, and floating over others that were in the heart of the present channel, we came to Dekorra, some seven miles below Portage. Dekorra is a quaint little hamlet, with just five weather-worn houses and a blacksmith-shop in sight, nestled in a hollow at the base of a bluff on the southern bank. The river courses at its feet, and from the top of a naked cliff a ferry-wire stretches high above the stream and loses itself among the trees on the opposite bottoms. The east wind whistled a pretty note as it was split by the swaying thread, and the anvil by the smith's forge rang out in unison, clear as a well-toned bell. A crude cemetery, apparently containing far more graves than Dekorra's present census would show inhabitants, flanks the faded-out settlement on the shoulder of an adjoining hill. The road to the tattered ferry-boat, rotting on the beach, gave but little evidence of recent use, for Dekorra is a relic.

The valley of the Wisconsin is from three to five miles broad, flanked on either side, below the Portage, by an undulating range of imposing bluffs, from one hundred and fifty to three hundred and fifty feet in height. They are heavily wooded, as a rule, although there is much variety,— pleasant grass-grown slopes ; naked, water-washed escarpments, rising sheer above the stream ; terraced hills, with eroded faces, ascending in a regular succession of benches to the cliff-like tops ; steep uplands, either covered with a dense and regular growth of forest, or shattered by fire or tornado. The ravines and pocket-fields between the bluffs are often of exceeding beauty, especially when occupied by a modest little village,— or better, by some small settler, whose outlet to the country beyond the edge of his mountain basin may be seen threading the woodlands which tower above him, or zigzagging through a neighboring pass, worn deep by some impatient spring torrent in a hurry to reach the river level.

Between these ranges stretches a wide expanse of bottoms, either bog or sand plain, over all of which the river flows at high water, and through which the swift current twists and bounds like a serpent in agony, constantly cutting out new channels and filling up the old, obeying laws of its own, ever defying the calculations of pilots and engineers. As it thus sweeps along, wherever its fancy listeth, here to-day and there to-morrow, it forms innumerable islands which greatly add to the picturesqueness of the view. Now and then there are two or three parallel channels, running along for miles before they join, perplexing the traveler with a labyrinth of water paths. These islands are often mere sand-bars, sometimes as barren as Sahara, again thick-grown with willows and seedling aspens; but for the most part they are well-wooded, their banks gay with the season's flowers, and luxuriant vines hanging in deep festoons from the trees which overhang the flood. At their heads, often high up among the branches of the elms, are great masses of driftwood, the remains of shattered lumber-rafts or saw-mill offal from the great northern pineries, evidencing the height of the spring flood which so often converts the Wisconsin into an Amazon.

Because of this spreading habit of the stream, the few villages along the way are planted on the higher land at the base of the bluffs, or on an occasional sandy pocket-plateau which the river, as in ages past it has worn its bed to lower levels, has left high and dry above present overflows. Some of these towns, in their fear of floods, are situated two or three miles back from the water highway; others, where the channel chances to closely hug a line of bluffs, are directly abutting the river, which is crossed at such points by either a ferry or a toll-bridge.

Desolate as is the prospect from Dekorra's front door, we found the limestone cliff there, a mine of attractiveness. The river has worn miniature caves and grottoes in its base; at the mouths of several of these there are little rocky beaches, whose overhanging walls are flecked with ferns, lichens, and graceful columbines.

At six o'clock that evening, in the midst of a dispiriting Scotch mist, we disembarked upon the northern bank, at the foot of a wooded bluff, and prepared to settle for the night. Fortunately, we had advance knowledge of the sparseness of settlement along the river, and had come with a tent and a cooking outfit, prepared for camping in case of need. Upon a rocky bench, fifty feet up from the water, we stretched a rope between two trees, to serve in lieu of a ridge-pole, and pitched our canvas domicile. It was a lonesome spot which we had chosen for our night's halt. Owing to the configuration of the bluffs, it was unlikely that any person dwelt within a mile of us on our shore. Across the valley, we looked over several miles of bottom woods, while far up on the opposite slopes could just be discerned the gables of two white farmhouses, peering out from a wilderness of trees stretching far and wide, till its limits were lost in the gathering fog.

It was pitchy dark by the time we had completed our camping arrangements, and W—— announced that the coffee was boiling over. I fancy we two must have presented a rather forlorn appearance, as we crouched at our evening meal around the sputtering little fire, clad in heavy jackets and rubber coats, for the atmosphere was raw and clammy. The wood was wet, and the shifting gusts would persist in blowing the smoke in our eyes, whichever position we took. Every falling bough, or rustle of a water-laden sapling, was suggestive of tramps or of inquisitive hogs or cattle, for we knew not what neighbors we had; many a time we paused, and peering out into the black night, listened intently for further developments. And then the strange noises from the river, unnoticed during daylight, were not conducive to mental ease, when we nervously associated them with roving fishermen, or perhaps tramps, attracted by our light from the opposite shore. Sometimes we felt positive that we heard the muffled creak of oars, fast approaching; then would come loud splashes and gurgles, and ever and anon it would seem as if some one were slapping the water with a board. Now near, now far away, approaching and receding by turns, these mysterious sounds continued through the night, occasionally relieved by moments of absolute silence. We afterward discovered that these were the customary refrains sung by the gay tide, as it washed over the wing-dams, swished around the sandbanks, and dashed against great snags and island heads.

But we did not know this then, and a certain uneasy lonesomeness overcame us as strangers to the scene; and I must confess that, despite our philosophizing, there was but little sleep for us that first camp out. A neglect to procure straw to soften our rocky couches, and a woful insufficiency of bed-clothing for a phenomenally cold August night, added to our manifold discomforts.

CHAPTER II.

THE LAST OF THE SACS.

DAWN came at five, and none too soon. But after thawing out over the breakfast fire and draining the coffee-pot dry, we were wondrously rejuvenated; and as we struck camp, were right merry between ourselves over the foolish nervousness of the night. There was still a raw northwest wind, but the clouds soon broke, and when, at half-past six, we again pushed out into the swift-flowing stream, it was evident that the day would be bright and comfortably cool.

We had some splendid vistas of bluff-girt scenery this morning, especially near Merrimac, where some of the elevations are the highest along the river. There are a score of houses at Merrimac, which is the point where the Chicago and Northwestern railway crosses, over an immense iron bridge 1736 feet long, spanning two broad channels and the sand island which divides them. The village is on a rolling plateau some fifty feet above the water level, on the northern side. Climbing up to the bridge-tender's house, that one-armed veteran of the spans, whose service here is as old as the bridge, told me that it was seldom indeed the river highway was used in these days. "The railroads kill this here water business," he said.

I found the tender to be something of a philosopher. Most bridge-tenders and fishermen, and others who pursue lonely occupations and have much spare time on their hands, are philosophers. That their speculations are sometimes cloudy does not detract from their local reputation of being deep thinkers. The Merrimac tender was given to geology, I found, and some of his ideas concerning the origin of the bluffs and the glacial streaks, and all that sort of thing, would create marked attention in any scientific journal. He had some original notions, too, about the habits of the stream above which he had almost hourly walked, day and night, the seasons round, for sixteen long years. The ice invariably commenced to form on the bottom of the river, he stoutly claimed, and then rose to the surface, — the ingenious reason given for this remarkable phenomenon being that the underlying sand was colder than the water. These and other novel results of his observation, our philosophical friend good-humoredly communicated, together with scraps of local tradition regarding the Black Hawk War, and lurid tales of the old lumber-raft days. At last, however, his hour came for walking the spans, and we descended to our boat. As we shot into the main channel, far above us a red flag fluttered from the draw, and we knew it to be the parting salute of the grizzled sentinel.

At the head of an island half a mile below, it is said there are the remains of an Indian fort. We landed with some difficulty, for the current sweeps by its wooded shore with particular zest. Our examination of the locality, however, revealed no other earth lines than might have been formed by a rushing flood. But as a reward for our endeavors, we found the lobelia cardinalis in wonderful profusion, mingled in striking contrast of color with the iron and sneeze weeds, and the common spurge. The prickly ash, with its little scarlet berry, was common upon this as upon other islands, and the elms were of remarkable size.

We were struck, as we passed along where the river chanced to wash the feet of steepy slopes, with the peculiar ridging of the turf. The water having undermined these banks, the friable soil upon their shoulders had slid, regularly breaking the sod into long horizontal strips a foot or two wide, the white sand gleaming between the rows of rusty green. Sometimes the shores were thus striped with zebra-like regularity for miles together, presenting a very singular and artificial appearance.

Prominent features of the morning's voyage, also, were deep bowlder-strewn and often heavily wooded ravines running down from the bluffs. Although perfectly dry at this season, it can be seen that they are the beds of angry torrents in the spring, and many a poor farmer's field is deeply cut with such gulches, which rapidly grow in this light soil as the years go on. We stopped at one such farm, and walked up the great breach to very near the house, up to which we clambered, over rocks and through sand-burrs and thickets, being met at the gate by a noisy dog, that appeared to be suspicious of strangers who approached his master's castle by means of the covered way. The farmer's wife, as she supplied us with exquisite dairy products, said that the metes and bounds of their little domain were continually changing; four acres of their best meadow had been washed out within two years, their wood-lot was being gradually undermined, and the ravine was eating into their ploughed land with the persistence of a cancer. On the other hand, her sister's acres, down the river a mile or two, on the other bank, were growing in extent. However, she thought their "luck would change one of these seasons," and the river swish off upon another tangent.

Upon returning by the gully, we found that its sunny, sloping walls, where not wooded with willows and oak saplings, were resplendent with floral treasures, chief among them being the gerardia, golden-rod in several varieties, tall white asters, a blue lobelia, and vervain, while the seeds of the Oswego tea, prairie clover, bed-straw, and wild roses were in all the glory of ripeness. There was a broad, pebbly beach at the base of the torrent's bed, thick-grown with yearling willows. A stranded pine-log, white with age and worn smooth by a generation of storms, lay firmly imbedded among the shingle. The temperature was still low enough to induce us to court the sunshine, and, leaning against this hoary castaway from the far North, we sat for a while and basked in the radiant smiles of Sol.

Prairie du Sac, thirty miles below Portage, is historically noted as the site for several generations of the chief village of the Sac Indians. Some of the earliest canoeists over this water-route, in the seventeenth and eighteenth centuries, describe the aboriginal community in some detail. The dilapidated white village of to-day numbers but four hundred and fifty inhabitants, — about one-fourth of the population assigned to the old red-skin town. The "prairie" is an oak-opening plateau, more or less fertile, at the base of the northern range of bluffs, which here takes a sudden sweep inland for three or four miles.

The Sacs had deserted this basin plain by the close of the eighteenth century, and taken up their chief quarters in the neighborhood of Rock Island, near the mouth of Rock River, in close proximity to their allies, the Foxes, who now kept watch and ward over the west bank of the Mississippi.

By a strange fatality it chanced that in the last days of July, 1832, the deluded Sac leader, Black Hawk, flying from the wrath of the Illinois and Wisconsin militiamen, under Henry and Dodge, chose this seat of the ancient power of his tribe to be one of the scenes of that fearful tragedy which proved the death-blow to Sac ambition. Black Hawk, after long hiding in the morasses of the Rock above Lake Koshkonong, suddenly flew from cover, hoping to cross the Wisconsin River at Prairie du Sac, and by plunging across the mountainous country over a trail known to the Winnebagoes, who played fast and loose with him as with the whites, to get beyond the Mississippi in quiet, as he had been originally ordered to do. His retreat was discovered when but a day old ; and the militiamen hurried on through the Jefferson swamps and the forests of the Four Lake country, harrying the fugitives in the rear. At the summit of the Wisconsin Heights, on the south bank, overlooking this old Sac plain on the north, Black Hawk and his rear-guard stood firm, to allow the women and children and the majority of his band of two thousand to cross the intervening bottoms and the island-strewn river. The unfortunate leader sat upon a white horse on the summit of the peak now called by his name, and shouted directions to his handful of braves. The movements of the latter were well executed, and Black Hawk showed good generalship ; but the militiamen were also well handled, and had superior supplies of ammunition, so when darkness fell the fated ravine and the wooded bottoms below were strewn with Indian bodies, and victory was with the whites. During the night the surviving fugitives, now ragged, foot-sore, and starving, crossed the river by swimming. A party of fifty or so, chiefly non-combatants, made a raft, and floated down the Wisconsin, to be slaughtered near its mouth by a detail of regulars and Winnebagoes from Prairie du Chien; but the mass of the party flying westward in hot haste over the prairie of the Sacs, headed for the Mississippi. They lined their rugged path with the dead and dying victims of starvation and despair, and a sorry lot these people were when the Bad Axe was finally reached, and the united army of regulars and militiamen under Atkinson, Henry, and Dodge, overtook them. The "battle" there was a slaughter of weaklings. But few escaped across the great river, and the bloodthirsty Sioux despatched nearly all of those.

Black Hawk was surrendered by the servile Winnebagoes, and after being exhibited in the Eastern cities, he was turned over to the besotted Keokuk for safe-keeping. He died, this last of the Sacs, poor, foolish old man, a few years later; and his bones, stolen for an Iowa museum, were cremated twenty years after in a fire which destroyed that institution. A sad history is that of this once famous people. We glory over the stately progress of the white man's civilization, but if we venture to examine with care the paths of that progress, we find our imperial chariot to be as the car of Juggernaut.

The view from the house verandas which overhang the high bank at Prairie du Sac, is superb. Eastward a half mile away, the grand, corrugated bluffs of Black Hawk and the Sugar Loaf tower to a height of over three hundred feet above the river level; while their lesser companions, heavily forested, continue the range, north and south, as far as the eye can reach. The river crosses the foreground with a majestic sweep, while for several miles to the west and southwest stretches the wooded plain, backed by a curved line of gloomy hills which complete the rim of the basin.

A mile below, on the same plain, is Sauk City, a shabby town of about a thousand inhabitants. A spur track of the Chicago, Milwaukee, and St. Paul railway runs up here from Mazomanie, crossing the river, which is nearly half a mile wide, on an iron bridge. A large and prosperous brewery appears to be the chief industry of the place. Slaughter-houses abut upon the stream, in the very centre of the village. These and the squalid back-door yards which run down to the bank do not make up an attractive picture to the canoeist. River towns differ very much in this respect. Some of them present a neat front to the water thoroughfare, with flower-gardens and well-kept yards and street-ends, while others regard the river as a sewer and the banks as a common dumping ground, giving the traveler by boat a view of filth, disorder, and general unsightliness which is highly repulsive. I have often found, on landing at some villages of this latter class, that the dwellings and business blocks which, riverward, are sad spectacles of foulness and unthrift, have quite pretentious fronts along the land highway which the townsfolk patronize. It is as if some fair dame, who prided herself on her manners and costume, had rags beneath her fine silks, and unwashed hands within her dainty gloves. This coming in at the back door of river towns reveals many a secret of sham.

It was a fine run down to Arena ferry, thirteen miles below Sauk City. The skies had become leaden and the atmosphere gray, and the sparse, gnarled poplars on some of the storm-swept bluffs had a ghostly effect. Here and there, fires had blasted the mountainous slopes, and a light aspen growth was hastening to garb with vivid green the blackened ruins. But the general impression was that of dark, gloomy forests of oak, linden, maple, and elms, on both upland and bottom; with now and then a noble pine cresting a shattered cliff.

There were fitful gleams of sunshine, during which the temperature was as high as could be comfortably tolerated; but the northwest wind swept sharply down through the ravines, and whenever the heavens became overcast, jackets were at once essential.

The islands became more frequent, as we progressed. Many of them are singularly beautiful. The swirling current gradually undermines their bases, causing the trees to topple toward the flood, with many graceful effects of outline, particularly when viewed above the island head. And the colors, too, at this season, are charmingly variegated. The sapping of a tree's foundations brings early decay; and the maples, especially, are thus early in the season gay with the autumnal tints of gold and wine and purple, objects of striking beauty for miles away. Under the arches of the toppling trees, and inside the lines of snags which mark the islet's former limits, the current goes swishing through, white with bubbles and dancing foam. Crouching low, to escape the twigs, one can have enchanting rides beneath these bowers, and catch rare glimpses of the insulated flora on the swift-passing banks. The stately spikes of the cardinal lobelia fairly dazzle the eye with their gleaming color; and great masses of brilliant yellow sneeze-weed and the deep purple of the iron-weed present a symphony which would delight a disciple of Whistler. Thus are the islands ever being destroyed and new ones formed. Those bottom lands, over there, where great forests are rooted, will have their turn yet, and the buffeted sand-bars of to-day given a restful chance to become bottoms. The game of shuttlecock and battledoor has been going on in this dark and awesome gorge since Heaven knows when. Man's attempt to control its movements seem puny indeed.

At six o'clock that evening we had arrived at the St. Paul railway bridge at Helena. The tender and his wife are a hospitable couple, and we engaged quarters in their cosy home at the southern end of the bridge. Mrs. P—— has a delightful flower-garden, which looks like an oasis in the wilderness of sand and bog thereabout. Twenty-three years ago, when these worthy people first took charge of the bridge, the earth for this walled-in beauty spot was imported by rail from a more fertile valley than the Wisconsin; and here the choicest of bulbs and plants are grown with rare floricultural skill, and the trainmen all along the division are resplendent in button-hole bouquets, the year round, products of the bridge-house bower at Helena. W—— and Mrs. P—— at once struck up an enthusiastic botanical friendship.

Bridge houses are generally most forlorn specimens of railway architecture, and have a barricaded look, as though tramps were altogether too frequent along the route, and occasionally made trouble for the watchers of the ties. This one, originally forbidding enough, has been transformed into a winsome vine-clad home, gay with ivies, Madeira vines, and passion, moon, and trumpet flowers, covering from view the professional dull green affected by "the company's" boss painter. The made garden, to one side, was choking with a wealth of bedding plants and greenhouse rarities of every hue and shape of blossom and leaf.

A dozen feet below the railroad level, spread wide morasses and sand patches, thick grown with swamp elms and willows. Down the track, a half mile to the south, Helena's fifty inhabitants are grouped in a dozen faded dwellings. Three miles westward, across the river, is the pretty and flourishing village of Spring Green.

It is needless to say that in the isolated home of these lovers of flowers, we had comfortable quarters. W—— said that it was very much like putting up at Rudder Grange.

CHAPTER III.

A PANORAMIC VIEW.

THE fog on the river was so thick, next morning, that objects four rods away were not visible. To navigate among the snags and shallows under such conditions was impossible. But W—— closely investigated the garden while waiting for the mist to rise, and Mr. P—— entertained me with intelligent reminiscences of his long experience here. It had been four years, he said, since he last swung the draw for a river craft. That was a small steamboat attempting to make the passage, on what was considered a good stage of water, from Portage to the mouth. She spent two weeks in passing from Arena to Lone Rock, a distance of twenty-two miles, and was finally abandoned on a sand-bank for the season. He doubted whether he would have occasion again to swing the great span. As for lumber rafts, but three or four small ones had passed down this year, for the railroads were transporting the product of the great mills on the Upper Wisconsin, about as cheap as it could be driven down river and with far less risk of disaster. The days of river traffic were numbered, he declared, and the little towns that had so long been supported by the raftsmen, on their long and weary journey from the northern pineries to the Hannibal and St. Louis markets, were dying of starvation.

I questioned our host as to his opinion of the value of the Fox-Wisconsin river improvement. He was cautious at first, and claimed that the money appropriated had "done a great deal of good to the poor people along the line." Closer inquiry developed the fact that these poor people had been employed in building the wing dams, for which local contracts had been let. When his opinion of the value of these dams was sought, Mr. P—— admitted that the general opinion along the river was, that they were "all nonsense," as he put it. Contracts had been let to Tom, Dick, and Harry, in the river villages, who had made a show of work, in the absence of inspectors, by sinking bundles of twigs and covering them with sand. Stone that had been hauled to the banks, to weight the mattresses, had remained unused for so long that popular judgment awarded it to any man who was enterprising enough to cart it away; thus was many a barn foundation hereabouts built out of government material. Sand-ballasted wing-dams built one season were washed out the next; and so government money has been recklessly frittered away. Such sort of management is responsible for the loose morality of the public concerning anything the general government has in hand. A man may steal from government with impunity, who would be socially ostracized for cheating his neighbor. There exists a popular sentiment along this river, as upon its twin, the Fox, that government is bound to squander about so much money every year in one way or another, and that the denizens of these two valleys are entitled to their share of the plunder. One honest captain on the Fox said to me, "If it wa'n't for this here appropriation, Wisconsin wouldn't get her proportion of the public money what each State is regularly entitled to; so I think it's necessary to keep this here scheme a-goin', for to get our dues; of course the thing ain't much good, so far as what is claimed for it goes, but it keeps money movin' in these valleys and makes times easier, — and that's what guvment's for." The honest skipper would have been shocked, probably, if I had called him a socialist, for a few minutes after he was declaiming right vigorously against Herr Most and the Chicago anarchists.

It was half-past nine before the warmth of the sun's rays had dissipated the vapor, and we ventured to set forth. It proved to be an enchanting day in every respect.

A mile or so below the bridge we came to the charming site, on the southern bank, at the base of a splendid limestone bluff, of the village of Old Helena, now a nameless clump of battered dwellings. There is a ferry here and a wooden toll-bridge in process of erection. The naked cliff, rising sheer above the rapid current, was, early in this century, utilized as a shot tower. There are lead mines some fifteen miles south, that were worked nearly fifty years before Wisconsin became even a Territory; and hither the pigs were, as late as 1830, laboriously drawn by wagons, to be precipitated down a rude stone shaft built against this cliff, and thus converted into shot. Much of the lead used by the Indians and white trappers of the region came from the Helena tower, and its product was in great demand during the Black Hawk War in 1832.

The remains of the shaft are still to be seen, although much overgrown with vines and trees.

Old Helena, in the earlier shot-tower days, was one of the "boom" towns of "the howling West." But the boom soon collapsed, and it was a deserted village even at the time of the Black Hawk disturbance. After the battle of Wisconsin Heights, opposite Prairie du Sac, the white army, now out of supplies, retired southwest to Blue Mound, the nearest lead diggings, for recuperation. Spending a few days there, they marched northwest to Helena. The logs and slabs which had been used in constructing the shanties here were converted into rafts, and upon them the Wisconsin was crossed, the operation consuming two days. A few miles north, Black Hawk's trail, trending westward to the Bad Axe, was reached, and soon after that came the final struggle.

We found many groups of pines, this morning, in the amphitheater between the bluffs, and under them the wintergreen berries in rich profusion. Some of the little pocket farms in these depressions are delightful bits of rugged landscape. In the fields of corn, now neatly shocked, the golden pumpkins seemed as if in imminent danger of rolling down hill. There are curious effects in architecture, where the barns and other outbuildings far overtop the dwellings, and have to be reached by flights of steps or angling paths. Yet here and there are pleasant, gently rolling fields, nearer the bank, and smooth, sugar-loaf mounds upon which cattle peacefully graze. The buckwheat patches are white with blossom. Now and then can just be distinguished the forms of men and women husking maize upon some fertile upland bench. And so goes on the day. Now, with pretty glimpses of rural life, often reminding one of Rhineland views, without the castles; then, swishing off through the heart of the bottoms for miles, shut in except from distant views of the hill-tops, and as excluded from humanity, in these vistas of sand and morass, as though traversing a wilderness; anon, darting past deserted rocky slopes or through the dark shadow of beetling cliffs, and the gloomy forests which crown them.

Lone Rock ferry is nearly fourteen miles below Helena bridge. As we came in view, the boat was landing a doctor's gig at the foot of a bold, naked bluff, on the southern bank. The doctor and the ferryman gave civil answers to our queries about distances, and expressed great astonishment when answered, in turn, that we were **bound for the** mouth of the river. "Mighty dull business," the doctor remarked, "traveling in that little cockle-shell; I should think you'd feel afraid, ma'am, on this big, lonesome river; my wife **don't** dare look **at** a boat, and I always feel skittish coming over on the ferry." I assured him that canoeing was far from being a dull business, and W—— good-humoredly added that she had as yet seen nothing to be afraid of. The doctor laughed and said something, **as he clicked** up his bony nag, about "**tastes** differing, anyhow." And, the ferryman trudging behind, — the smoke from his cabin chimney was rising above the tree-tops in a neighboring ravine, — the little cortege wound its way up the rough, angling roadway fashioned out of the face of the bluff, and soon vanished around a corner. Lone Rock village is a mile and a half inland to the south.

Just below, the cliff overhangs the stream, its base having been **worn into** by centuries of ceaseless washing. On a narrow beach beneath, a group of cows were chewing their cuds in an atmosphere of refreshing coolness. From the rocky roof above them hung ferns in many varieties, — maidenhair, the wood, the sensitive, and the bladder; while in clefts and grottos, or amid great heaps of rock debris, hard by, there were generous masses of king fern, lobelia cardinalis, iron and sneeze weed, golden-rod, daisies, closed gentian, and eupatorium, in startling contrasts of vivid color. It being high noon, we stopped and landed at this bit of fairy land, ate our dinner, and botanized. There was a tinge of triumphant scorn in W——'s voice, when, emerging from a spring-head grotto, bearing in one arm a brilliant bouquet of wild flowers and in the other a mass of fern fronds, she cried, "To think of his calling canoeing a dull business!"

Richland City, on the northern bank, five miles down, is a hamlet of fifteen or twenty houses, some of them quite neat in appearance. Nestled in a grove of timber on a plain at the base of the bluffs, the village presents a quaint old-country appearance for a long distance up-stream. The St. Paul railway, which skirts the northern bank after crossing the Helena bridge, sends out a spur northward from Richland City, to Richland Center, the chief town in Richland county.

Two miles below Richland City, we landed at the foot of an imposing bluff, which rises sharply for three hundred feet or more from the water's edge. It is practically treeless on the river side. We ascended it through a steep gorge washed by a spring torrent. Strewn with bowlders and hung with bushes and an occasional thicket of elms and oaks, the path was rough but sure. From the heights above, the dark valley lay spread before us like a map. Ten miles away, to our left, a splash of white in a great field of green marked the location of Lone Rock village; five miles to the right, a spire or two rising above the trees indicated where Muscoda lay far back from the river reaches; while in front, two miles away, peaceful little Avoca was sunning its gray roofs on a gently rising ground. Between these settlements and the parallel ranges which hemmed in the panoramic view, lay a wide expanse of willow-grown sand-fields, forested morasses, and island meadows through which the many-channeled river cut its devious way. In the middle foreground, far below us, some cattle were being driven through a bushy marsh by boys and dogs. The cows looked the size of kittens to us at our great elevation, but such was the purity of the atmosphere that the shouts and yelps of the drivers rose with wonderful clearness, and the rustling of the brush was as if in an adjoining lot. The noise seemed so disproportioned to the size of the objects occasioning it, that **this acoustic** effect was at first rather startling.

The whitewashed cabin of a squatter and his few log outbuildings **occupy** a little basin to one side **of** the bluff. **His** cattle were ranging over the hillsides, attend**ed** by a colly. The family were rather neatly dressed, but there did not appear to be over **an acre** of land level enough for cultivation, and **that was** entirely devoted to Indian corn. It was something of a mystery how this man could earn a living in his cooped-up mountain home. **But** the honest-looking fellow **seemed** quite contented, sitting in the shade **of** his woodpile smoking a corncob pipe, **surrounded by a** half dozen children. He cheerfully responded **to** my few queries, as we stopped at his **well on** the **return** to our boat. The good wife, a buxom woman with pretty blue eyes set in a smiling **face,** was peeling a pan of potatoes on the porc**h, near** by, while one foot rocked a rude cradle ingeniously formed out **of** a barrel head and a lemon box. She seemed mightily pleased as W—— stroked the face of the chubby infant within, and made inquiries as to the ages of the step-laddered brood ; and the father, **too,** fairly beamed with satisfaction as he placed **his** hands on the golden curls of his two oldest misses and proudly exhibited their little tricks of precocity. There can be no poverty under such a roof. Millionnaires might well envy the peaceful contentment of these hillside squatters.

Down to Muscoda we followed the rocky and wood-crowned northern bank, along which the country highway is cut out. The swift current closely hugs it, and there was needed but slight exertion with the paddles to lead a sewing-machine agent, whom we found to be urging his horse into a vain attempt to distance the canoe. As he seemed to court a race, we had determined not to be outdone, and were not.

Orion, on the northern side, just above Muscoda, is a deserted town. It must have been a pretentious place at one time. There are a dozen empty business buildings, now tenanted by bats and spiders. On one shop front, a rotting sign displays the legend, "World's Exchange;" there is also a "Globe Hotel," and the remains of a bank or two. Alders, lilacs, and gnarled apple-trees in many deserted clumps, tell where the houses once were; and the presence, among these ruins, of a family or two of squalid children only emphasizes the dreary loneliness. Orion was once a "boom" town, they tell us, — an expressive epitaph.

A thin, outcropping substratum of sandstone is noticeable in this section of the river. It underlies the sandy plains which abut the Wisconsin in the Muscoda region, and lines the bed of the stream; near the banks, where there is but a slight depth of water, rapids are sometimes noticeable, the rocky bottom being now and then scaled off into a stairlike form, for the fall is here much sharper than customary.

Because of an outlying shelf of this sandstone, bordered by rapids, but covered with only a few inches of dead water, we had some difficulty in landing at Muscoda beach, on the southern shore. Some stout poling and lifting were essential before reaching land. Muscoda was originally situated on the bank, which rises gently from the water; but as the river trade fell off, the village drifted up nearer the bluff, a mile south over the plain, in order to avoid the spring floods. There is a toll-bridge here and a large brewery, with extensive cattle-sheds strung along the shore. A few scattering houses connect these establishments with the sleepy but neat little hamlet of some five hundred inhabitants. After a brisk walk up town, in the fading sunlight, which cast a dazzling glimmer on the whitened dunes and heightened the size of the dwarfed herbage, we returned to the canoe, and cast off to seek camping quarters for the night, down-stream.

A mile below, on the opposite bank, a large straw-stack by the side of a small farmhouse attracted our attention. We stopped to investigate. There was a good growth of trees upon a gentle slope, a few rods from shore, and a beach well strewn with drift-wood. The farmer who greeted us was pleasant-spoken, and readily gave us permission to pitch our tent in the copse and partake freely of his straw.

Now more accustomed to the river's ways, we keenly enjoyed our supper, seated around our little camp-fire in the early dark. We had occasional glimpses of the lights in Muscoda, through the swaying trees on the bottoms to the south; an owl, on a neighboring island, incessantly barked like a terrier; the whippoorwills were sounding their mournful notes from over the gliding river, and now and then a hoarse grunt or querulous squeal in the wood-lot behind us gave notice that we were quartered in a hog pasture. Soon the moon came out and brilliantly lit the opens, — the glistening river, the stretches of white sand, the farmer's fields, — and intensified the sepulchral shadows of the lofty bluffs which overhang the scene.

CHAPTER IV.

FLOATING THROUGH FAIRYLAND.

UNDISTURBED by hogs or river tramps, we slept soundly until seven, the following morning. There was a heavy fog again, but by the time we had leisurely eaten our breakfast, struck camp, and had a pleasant chat with our farmer host and his "hired man," who had come down to the bank to make us a call, the mists had rolled away before the advances of the sun.

At half past ten we were at Port Andrew, eight miles below camp on the north shore. The Port, or what is left of it, lies stretched along a narrow bench of sand, based with rock, some forty feet above the water, with a high, naked bluff backing it to the north. There is barely room for the buildings, on either side of its one avenue paralleling the river; this street is the country road, which skirts the bank, connecting the village with the sparse settlements, east and west. In the old rafting days, the Port was a stopping-place for the lumber pilots. There being neither rafts nor pilots, nowadays, there is no business for the Port, except what few dollars may be picked up from the hunters who frequent this place each fall, searching for woodcock. But even the woodcocking industry has been overdone here, and two sportsmen whom we met on the beach declared that there were not enough birds remaining to pay for the trouble of getting here. For, indeed, Port Andrew is quite off the paths of modern civilization. There is practically no communication with the country over the bluffs, northward; and Blue River, the nearest railway station, to which there is a tri-weekly mail, is four miles southward, over the bottoms, with an uncertain ferryage between. There are less than fifty human beings in Port Andrew now, but double that number of dogs, the latter mostly of the pointer breed, kept for the benefit of huntsmen.

We climbed the bank and went over to the post-office and general store. It seems to be the only business establishment left alive in the hamlet; although there are a dozen deserted buildings which were stores in the long ago, but are now ghostly wrecks, open to wind and weather on every side, and, with sunken ridge-poles, waiting for the first good wind-storm to furnish an excuse for a general collapse. A sleepy, greasy-looking lad, whose originally white shirt-front was sadly stained with water-melon juice, had charge of the meager concern. He said that the farmers north of the bluffs traded in towns more accessible than this, and that south of the stream, Blue River, being a railroad place, was "knockin' the spots off 'n the Port." Ten years ago, he had heard his "pa" say the Port was "a likely place," but it "ain't much shakes now."

But there is a certain quaintness about these ruins of Port Andrew that is quite attractive. A deep ravine, cut through the shale-rock, comes winding down from a pass among the bluffs, severing the hamlet in twain. Over it there is sprung a high-arched, rough stone bridge, with crenelled walls, quite as artistic in its way as may be found in pictures of ancient English brook-crossings. On the summit of a rising-ground beyond, stands the solitary, whitened skeleton of a once spacious inn, a broad double-decked veranda stretching across its river front, and hitching-posts and drinking-trough now almost lost to view in a jungle of docks and sand-burrs.

The cracks in the rotten veranda floors are lined with grass; the once broad highway is now reduced to an unfrequented trail through the yielding sand, which is elsewhere hid under a flowery mantle made up of delicate, fringed blossoms of pinkish purple, called by the natives "Pike's weed," and the rich yellow and pale gold of the familiar "butter and eggs." The peculiar effect of color, outline, and perspective, that hazy August day, was indeed charming. But we were called from our rapt contemplation of the picture, by the assemblage around us of half the population of Port Andrew, led by the young postmaster and accompanied by a drove of playful hounds. The impression had somehow got abroad that we had come to prospect for an iron mine, in the bed of the old ravine, and there was a general desire to see how the thing was done. The popular disappointment was evidently great, when we descended from our perch on the old bridge wall, and returned to the little vessel on the beach, which had meanwhile been closely overhauled by a knot of inquisitive urchins. A part of the crowd followed us down, plying innocent questions by the score, while on the summit of the bank above stood a watchful group of women and girls, some in huge sun-bonnets, others with aprons thrown over their heads. There was a general **waving of hats** and aprons from the shore, as we shot off **into** the current again, and our "**Good-by!**" **was** answered **by a** cheery chorus. It is evident that Port **Andrew** does not have many exciting episodes in her aimless, far-away life.

Flocks of crows were seen to-day, winging their funereal flight from shore **to shore, and** uttering dismal croaks. The islands presented a more luxurious flora than we had yet seen; the marsh grass upon them **was** rank and tall, the overhanging trees sumptuously vine-clad, the autumn **tints** deeper and richer than before, the banks glowing with cardinal and yellow and purple; while on the sandy shores we saw loosestrife, white asters, the sensitive plant, golden-rod, and button-bush. **Blue** herons drifted through the air on their **wide-spread** wings, heads curved back upon their shoulders, and legs hanging straight down, to settle at last upon barren sand-spits, and stand in silent contemplation of some pool of dead water where perhaps a stray fish might reward their watchfulness. Solitary kingfishers kept their vigils on the numerous snags. Now and then **a turtle** shuffled from his perch and went tumbling with a loud splash into his favorite watering-place.

Although yet too early for Indian summer, the day became, by noon, very like those which are the delight of a protracted northwestern autumn. A golden haze threw a mystic veil over the landscape; distant shore lines were obliterated, sand and sky and water at times merged in an indistinct blur, and distances were deceptive. Now and then the vistas of white sand-fields would apparently stretch on to infinity. Again, the river would seem wholly girt with cliffs and we in the bottom of a huge mountain basin, from which egress was impossible; or the stream would for a time appear a boundless lake. The islands ahead were as if floating in space, and there were weird reflections of far-away objects in the waters near us. While these singular effects lasted we trimmed our bark to the swift-gliding current, and floated along through fairy-land, unwilling to break the charm by disturbing the mirrored surface of the flood.

Soon after the dinner hour we came in sight of the Boscobel toll-bridge, — an ugly, clumsy structure, housed-in like a tunnel, and as dark as a pocket. I was never quite able to understand why some bridge-makers should cover their structures in this fashion, and others, in the same locality, leave them open to wind and weather. So far as my unexpert observation goes, covered bridges are no more durable than the open, and they are certainly less cheerful and comely. A chill always comes over me as I enter one of these damp and gloomy hollow-ways; and the thought of how well adapted they are to the purposes of the thug or the footpad is not a particularly pleasant one for the lonely traveler by night. A dead little river hamlet, now in abject ruins, — Manhattan by name, — occupies the rugged bank at the north end of the long bridge; while southward, Boscobel is out of sight, a mile and a half inland, across the bottoms. The bluff overtopping Manhattan is a quarry of excellent hard sandstone, and a half dozen men were dressing blocks for shipment, on the rocky shore above us. They and their families constitute Manhattan.

Eight miles down river, also on the north bank, is Boydtown. There are two houses there, in a sandy glen at the base of a group of heavily wooded foot-hills. At one of the dwellings — a neat, slate-colored cottage — we found a cheery, black-eyed woman sitting on the porch with a brood of five happy children playing about her. As she hurried away to get the butter and milk which we had asked for, she apologized for being seen to enjoy this unwonted leisure, apparently not desirous that we should suppose her to be any other than the hard-working little body which her hands and driving manner proclaimed her to be. When she returned with our supplies she said that they had "got through thrashin'," the day before, and she was enjoying the luxury of a rest preparatory to an accumulated churning. I looked incredulously at the sandy waste in which this little home was planted, and the good woman explained that their farm lay farther back, on fair soil, although the present dry season had not been the best for crops.

Her brown-faced boy of ten and two little girls of about eight — the laughing faces and crow-black curls of the latter hid under immense flapping sun-bonnets — accompanied us to the bayou by which we had approached Boydtown. They had a gay, unrestrained manner that was quite captivating, and we were glad to have them row alongside of us for a way down-stream in the unwieldy family punt, the lad handling the crude oars and the girls huddled together on the stern seat, covered by their great sun-bonnet flaps, as with a cape. They were "goin' grapein'," they said; and at an island where the vines hung dark with purple clusters, they piped "Good-by, you uns!" in tittering unison.

By this time, the weather had changed. The haze had lifted. The sky had quickly become overcast with leaden rainclouds, and an occasional big drop gave warning of an approaching storm. A few miles below Boydtown, we stopped to replenish our canteen at the St. Paul railway's fine iron bridge, the last crossing on that line between Milwaukee and Prairie du Chien. On the southern end of the bridge is Woodman; on the northern bank, the tender's house. As we were in the northern channel, it was impracticable to reach the village, separated from us by wide islands and long stretches of swamp and forest, except by walking the bridge and the mile or two of trestle-work approaches to the south. As for the bridge-house, there chanced to be no spare quarters for us there. So we voted to trust to fortune and push on, although the tender's wife, a pleasant, English-faced woman, with black, sparkling eyes and a hospitable smile, was much exercised in spirit, and thought we were running some hazard of a wetting.

The skies lightened for a time, and then there came rolling up from over the range to the southwest great jagged rifts of black clouds, ugly "thunder heads," which seemed to presage a deluge. Below them, veiling the tallest peaks, tossed and sped the light-footed couriers of the wind, and we saw the dark-green bosom of the upper forests heave with the emotions of the air, while the rushing stream below flowed on unruffled. The river is here united in one broad channel. At the first evidence of a blow, we hurried across to the windward bank. We were landing at the swampy, timber-strewn base of a precipitous cliff as the wind passed over the valley, and had just completed our preparations for shelter when the rain began to come in blinding sheets.

The possibility of having to spend the night under the sepulchral arches of this forested morass was not pleasant to contemplate. The storm abated, however, within half an hour, and we were then able to distinguish a large white house apparently set back in an open field a half mile or more from the opposite shore.

Re-embarking, we headed that way, and found a wood-fringed stream several rods wide, pouring a vigorous flood into the Wisconsin, from the north. Our map showed it to be the Kickapoo, an old-time logging river, and the house must be an outlying member of the small railroad village of Wauzeka. A consultation was held on board, at the mouth of the Kickapoo. On the Wisconsin not a house was to be seen, as far as the eye could reach, and wide stretches of swamp and wooded bog appeared to line both its banks. The prospect of paddling **up** the mad little Kickapoo for a mile to Wauzeka was dispiriting, but we decided to do **it**; for night was coming on, our tent, even could we find a good camping ground in this marshy wilderness, was disposed to be leaky, and a steady drizzle continued to sound a muffled tattoo on our rubber coats. A voluble fisherman, caught out in the rain like ourselves, came swinging into the tributary, with his cranky punt, just as we were setting our paddles for a vigorous pull up-stream. We **had his com**pany, side by side, till we reached the St. Paul railway trestle, and beached at the foot of a deserted stave mill, in whose innermost recesses we deposited our traps. Guided by the village shoemaker's boy, who had been playing by the river side, we started up the track to find the hotel, nearly a half mile away.

It is a quiet, comfortable, old-fashioned **lit**tle inn, this hostelry at Wauzeka. The landlord greeted his storm-bound guests with polite urbanity, and with none of that inquisitiveness so common in rural hosts. **At sup-**

per, we met the village philosopher, a quaint, lone old man who has an opinion of his own upon most human subjects, and more than dares to voice it,—insists, in fact, on having it known of all men. A young commercial traveler, the only other patron of the establishment, sadly guyed our philosophical messmate by securing his verdict on a wide range of topics, from the latest league game to abstruse questions of theology. The philosopher bit, and the drummer was in high feather as he crinkled the corners of his mouth behind his huge moustache, and looked slyly around for encouragement that was not offered.

Wauzeka is, in one respect, like too many other country villages. Three saloons disfigure the main street, and in front of them are little knots of noisy loafers, in the evening, filling up the rickety, variously graded sidewalk to the gutter, and necessitating the running of a loathsome gauntlet to those who may wish to pass that way. The boy who can grow up in such an atmosphere, unpolluted, must be of rare material, or his parents exceptionally judicious. There are few large cities where one can see the liquor traffic carried on with such disgusting boldness as in hamlets like this, where screenless, open-doored saloons of a vile character **jostle** trading shops and dwellings, and monopolize the footway, making **of the** business street a place which women may **abhor at** any hour, and must necessarily **avoid** after sunset. With a local-option law, that but awaits **a** majority vote to be operative in **such** communities, **it is** a strange commentary on the quality of our nineteenth-century civilization **that the** dissolute few should still, as of old, be able to persistently hold the whip-hand over the **virtuous** but timid many.

Elsewhere in Wauzeka, there are many pretty grass-grown lanes; some substantial cottages; a prosperous creamery, employing the service of the especial pride of the village, a six-inch spouting well, driven for three hundred feet to the underlying stratum of limerock; a saw-mill or two, which are worked spasmodically, according to the log-driving stage in the Kickapoo, and some pleasant, accommodating people, who appear to be quite contented with their lot in life.

CHAPTER V.

THE DISCOVERY OF THE MISSISSIPPI.

THERE was fog on the river in the morning. Across the broad expanse of field and ledge which separates Wauzeka from the Wisconsin, we could see the great white mass of vapor, fifty feet thick, resting on the broad channel like a dense coverlid of down. Soon after seven o'clock, the cloud lifted by degrees, and then broke into ragged segments, which settled sluggishly for a while on the tops of the southern line of bluffs and screened their dark amphitheaters from view, till at last dissipated into thin air.

We were off at eight o'clock, fifteen or twenty men coming down to the railway-bridge to watch the operation. One of them helped us materially with our bundles, while the rest sat in a row along the trestle, dangling their feet through the spaces between the stringers, and gazing at us as though we were a circus company on the move. A drizzle set in, just as we pushed from the bank, and we descended the Kickapoo under much the same conditions of atmosphere as those we had experienced in pulling against its swirling tide the evening before.

But by nine o'clock the storm was over, and we had, for a time, a calm, quiet journey, a gray light which harmonized well with the wildly picturesque scenery, and a fresh west breeze which helped us on our way. We were now but twenty miles from the mouth. The parallel ranges of bluff come nearer together, until they are not much over a mile apart, and the stream, now broader, swifter, and deeper, is less encumbered with islands. Upon the peaty banks are the tall white spikes of the curious turtlehead, occasional masses of balsam-apple vines, the gleaming lobelia cardinalis, yellow honeysuckles just going out of blossom, and acres of the golden sneezeweed, which deserves a better name.

At Wright's Ferry, ten miles below, there are domiciled two German families, and on the shore is a saw-mill which is operated in the spring, to work up the logs which farmers bring down from the gloomy mountains which back the scene.

Bridgeport, four miles farther, — still on the

northern side,— is chiefly a clump of little red railway buildings set up on a high bench carved from the face of the bluff, their fronts resting on the road-bed and their rears on high scaffolding. A few big bowlders rolling down from the cliffs would topple Bridgeport over into the river. There is a covered country toll-bridge here, and the industrial interest of the Liliputian community is quarrying. It is the last hamlet on the river.

A mist again formed, casting a blue tinge over the peaks and giving them a far distant aspect; dark clouds now and then lowered and rolled through the upper ravines, reflecting their inky hue upon the surface of the deep, gliding river. The bluffs, which had for many miles closely abutted the stream, at last gradually swept away to the north and south, to become part of the great wall which forms the eastern bulwark of the Upper Mississippi. At their base spreads a broad, flat plain, fringed with boggy woods and sandy meadows, the delta of the Wisconsin, which, below the Lowertown bridge of the Burlington and Northern railway, is cut up into flood-washed willow islands, flanked by a wide stretch of shifting sand-bars black with tangled roots and stranded logs, the debris of many a spring-time freshet.

It was about half-past twelve o'clock when we came to the junction of the Wisconsin and the Mississippi. Upon a willow-grown sand-reef edging the swamp, which extends northward for five miles to the quaint, ancient little city of Prairie du Chien, a large barge lies stranded. A lone fisherman sat upon its bulwark rail, which overhangs the rushing waters as they here commingle. We landed with something akin to reverence, for this must have been about the place where Joliet and Marquette, two hundred and fourteen years ago, gazed with rapture upon the mighty Mississippi, which they had at last discovered, after so many thousands of miles of arduous journeying through a savage-haunted wilderness. And indeed it is an imposing sight. To the west, two miles away, rise the wooded peaks on the Iowa side of the great river. Northward there are pretty glimpses of cliffs and rocky beaches through openings in the heavy growth which covers the islands of the upper stream. Southward is a long vista of curving hills and glinting water shut in by the converging ranges. Eastward stretches the green delta of the Wisconsin, flanked by those imposing bluffs, between whose bases for two centuries has flowed a curious throng of humanity, savage and civilized, on errands sacred and profane, representing many clashing nationalities.

The rain descended in a gentle shower as I was lighting a fire on which to cook our last canoeing meal of the season; and W—— held an umbrella over the already damp kindling in order to give it a chance. We no doubt made a comical picture as we crouched together beneath this shelter, jointly trying to fan the sparks into a flame, for the fisherman, who had been heretofore speechless, and apparently rapt in his occupation, burst out into a hearty laugh. When we turned to look at him he hid his face under his upturned coat-collar, and giggled to himself like a school-girl. He was a jolly dog, this fisherman, and after we had presented him with a cup of coffee and what solids we could spare from our now meager store, he warmed into a very communicative mood, and gave us much detailed, though rather highly colored, information about the locality, especially as to its natural features.

The rain had ceased by the time dinner was over; so we bade farewell to the happy fisherman and the presiding deities of the Wisconsin, and pulled up the giant Mississippi to Prairie du Chien, stopping on our way to visit an out-of-the-way bayou, botanically famous,

The Discovery of the Mississippi.

where flourishes the rare nelumbium luteum, — America's nearest approach to the lotus of the Nile.

And thus was accomplished the season's stint of six hundred miles of canoeing upon the Historic Waterways of Illinois and Wisconsin.

INDEX.

ALGOMA, 182, 186.
Allouez, Father Claude, 176, 228, 229.
American Fur Co., 145.
Anderson, Maj. Robert, U.S.A., 19.
Antoinette, Marie, Queen of France, 224.
Appleton, Wis., 23, 27, 185, 202-207, 209.
Arena Ferry, Wis., 27, 257, 262.
Arndt, Judge John P., 158.
Astor, John Jacob, 145, 232.
Atkinson, Gen. Henry, U. S. A., 19, 255.
Avoca, Wis., 270.

BAD AXE, battle of, 255, 266.
Baraboo River, 241.
Barth, Laurent, 143.
Beloit, Wis., 20, 26, 65.
Berlin, Wis., 21, 22, 27, 164, 173-175, 177, 240.
Black Hawk War, 18, 19, 87, 119, 252, 253-255, 266.
Black Hawk Mountain, 256.
Black River Falls, Wis., 200.
Black Wolf Point, Lake Winnebago, 191.
Blue Mound, Wis., 266.
Blue River Village, Wis., 276.
Boscobel, Wis., 27, 280, 281.
"Bourbon, The American." *See* Williams, Eleazar.

Boydtown, Wis., 27, 281, 282.
Bridgeport, Wis., 27, 289, 290.
Buffalo Lake, 22, 160-162, 168, 173.
Butte des Morts, Lake Grand, 161, 181-183, 199.
Butte des Morts, Lake Petit, 199, 201, 202.
Butte des Morts Village, 183-185, 188.
Butterfield, Consul W., *cited*, 176.
Byron, Ill., 19, 26, 82-85.

CANOEING, pleasures of, 15, 16.
Canoeists, suggestions to, 23-26.
Canoes, styles of, 15, 16.
Carbon Cliff, Ill., 138, 139.
Catfish River, Wis., 18, 31-59.
Champche Keriwinke, Winnebago princess, 200, 201.
Champlain, Governor of Quebec, 175, 230.
Cherry River, 80.
Chicago, Burlington, and Northern Ry., 290.
Chicago, Burlington, and Quincy Ry., 137-139.
Chicago, Milwaukee, and St. Paul Ry., 76, 82, 178, 186, 256, 259-265, 269, 283, 285.
Chicago and Northwestern Ry., 65, 248-250.
Cleveland, Ill., 137.

Index.

Coloma, Ill., 26, 138-140.
Como, Ill., 26, 109-111.
Crooks, Ramsay, 232.

DABLON, Father Claude, 229.
Dakotah Indians. *See* Sioux and Winnebagoes.
Davis, Jefferson, 19, 145, 146.
Dekorra, Wis., 242-245.
De Korra, early fur trader, 199, 200.
Depere, Wis., 206, 225, 228, 229.
Dixon, Ill., 18, 20, 26, 87, 93, 94, 97-101, 106-108.
Dodge, Maj. Henry, 253, 255.
Doty's Island, Wis., 195-201.
Dunkirk, Wis., 52, 53.

ERIE, Ill., 26, 124-136.
Eureka, Wis., 178.

FIRST LAKE, 40, 43-45.
Fond du Lac, Wis., 191.
Fort Crawford (Prairie du Chien, Wis.), 145.
Fort Howard, Wis., 145, 228-234.
Fort Winnebago (Portage, Wis.), 144-146.
FourLake country, Wis., 18, 33, 254.
Four Legs, Winnebago chief, 200, 201.
Fox Indians (*see*, also, Sacs), 176, 196-199.
Fox River, Wis., 17, 21-23, 26, 141-234, 239, 240, 255.
Fulton, Wis., 56-58.
Fur trade in Wisconsin, 189, 196-200, 207, 208, 231, 234.

GANYMEDE SPRINGS, Ill., 89, 90.
Garlic Island, Lake Winnebago, 189-191.
Garritty, Mary, 226-228.
Grand Detour, Ill., 92-106.
Great Bend of Rock River, 105-106.
Green Bay, Wis., 23, 27, 180, 181, 185, 198, 207, 229-234, 238.
Grignon, Augustin, 184, 185, 188, 232.

HANSON, John H., *cited*, 224, 225.
Harney, Gen. William S., U. S. A., 145.
Helena Village, Wis, 27, 259-265.
Helena, Wis., Old, 265, 266.
Henry, Maj. James D, 253, 255.
Hoo-Tschope. *See* Four Legs.

ILLINOIS INDIANS, 21, 176.
Iowatuk, Winnebago princess, 189, 191.

JANESVILLE, Wis., 20, 26, 60-65.
Jesuit missionaries, 21, 24, 176, 177, 180, 181, 228, 229, 231.
Joliet, Sieur de, 21, 176, 229, 239.

KACKALIN, Grand. *See* Kaukauna.
Kaukauna, Wis., 27, 185, 206-213.
Kellogg's trail, 106, 107.
Keokuk, Fox chief, 255.
Kickapoo Indians, 175.
Kickapoo River, Wis., 27, 284, 285, 287, 288.
Kinzie, Mrs. John H., *cited*, 146, 200.
Koshkonong, Lake, 18, 19, 59, 254.

LAKESIDE, Third Lake, 32.
Langlade, Charles de, 198, 232.
Latham Station, Ill., 76, 77.
Lawrence University, 205, 206.
Lead mines at Galena, 18.
Lecuyer, Jean B., 143, 144.
Lignery, Sieur Marchand de, 198.
Lincoln, Abraham, 19.
Little Kaukauna, Wis., 206, 216-219, 221, 225.
Lone Rock, Wis., 27, 262, 267-270.
Louis XVI., King of France, 223-225.
Louis XVII., Dauphin of France, 223-225.
Louvigny, Sieur de, 198.
Lyndon, Ill., 26, 118.

MADISON, Wis., 18, 26.

Manhattan, Wis., 281.
Marin, Sieur de, 197, 198.
Marquette, Father James, **21, 157,** 176, 229, 239
Marquette Village, Wis., **26, 161,** 166-170.
Mascoutin Indians, 175-178.
Mazomanie, Wis., 256.
Menasha, Wis., 23, 183, **185, 195, 196, 207.**
Menomonee Indians, 187, **188, 196,** 197, 223.
Merrimac, Wis., 27, 248-250.
Miami Indians, 175.
Milan, Ill., 139.
Milwaukee and Northern Ry., 203, 204.
Mississippi River, 21, **26, 27,** 136, 138, 180, 229-231, 239, 253-255, 290-293.
Mohawk Indians, 222.
Montello, Wis., 22, 26, **160, 162-** 164, 168.
Muscoda, Wis., 23, 27, 270, **272-** 274.

NEENAH, Wis., 22, **27, 183, 185,** 191, 195-201, 206.
New York Indians. *See* Oneidas.
Nicolet, Jean, 21, 175, 176, **230,** 231.
Northern Insane Hospital, Wis., **189-191.**

OMRO, Wis., 22, **27,** 175, **178, 179.**
Oneida Indians, 222-228.
Oregon, Ill., 20, 26, 83-90.
Orion, Wis., 272.
Oshkosh, Menomonee chief, 187, 188.
Oshkosh, Wis., 27, 161, **182, 183,** 185-188, 190, 207.
Ott's Farm, Madison, Wis., 33.
Owen, Ill. *See* Latham Station.

PACKWAUKEE, Wis., 26, 150, 157-161, 163.
Paine Bros., 186.
Paquette, Pierre, 144.

Penney, Josephine, 226-228.
Philippe, Louis, King of France, **225.**
Pope's Springs, Wis., 60.
Porlier, James, 184, 185.
Porlier, Louis B., 184, 185.
Portage, Wis., 21, 23, 26, 27, 143-146, **160, 161,** 185, 198, 206, 237-**242.**
Port Andrew, Wis., 27, 275-279.
Pottawattomie Indians, 18, 19, 87.
Poygan Lake, **22, 180, 181.**
Prairie du **Chien, Wis., 21, 27,** 145, 238, 240, 255, **291-293.**
Prairie du Sac, **Wis., 23, 27, 252-** 256, 266.
Princeton, Wis., **22, 27, 168-172, 210.**
Prophetstown, Ill., **18,** 26, **118-120.**
Puckawa Lake, 22, 161, 163-169.

RED BIRD, Winnebago chief, **145.**
Richland Center, Wis., 269.
Richland City, Wis., 269.
Rockford, Ill., **20,** 26, **79.**
Rock Island, Ill., **18, 26,** 139, 140, 253.
Rock **River, 17-21, 29-140, 213,** 253.
Rockton, Ill., **20.**
Roscoe, Ill., 74, **76.**

SAC INDIANS, **18, 19,** 119, 198, 253-256.
Sacramento, Wis., 177, 178.
Sauk City, Wis., 23, 256, 257.
Sawyer, Philetus, 186.
Second Lake, 33, 36-39, 43.
Shaubena, Pottawattomie chief, 18.
Sioux Indians, 230, 231, 255.
Smith's Island, Wis., 149-156.
Spring Green, Wis., 261.
Stebbinsville, Wis., 53, 54.
Sterling, Ill., 20, 26, 108, 109.
Stillman's Creek, 19, 83, 86, 87.
Stillman's defeat, 19, 87.
Stoughton, Wis., 20, **26, 42, 44,** 46-50, 52.
Stuart, Robert, 232.

TAYLOR, Zachary, 19.
Third Lake, 31, 33.
Turvill's Bay, Third Lake, 32, **33.**
Twiggs, Maj. David, 232.

WALKING CLOUD, a Winnebago, 200.
Wauzeka, Wis., 27, 285-288.
White Cloud, Indian prophet, 18, 119.
White River lock, 172, 173.
Williams, Eleazar, 222-228.
Williams, Mrs. Eleazar, **225, 226.**
Winnebago Indians, 19, 119, 145, 166, 189, 196, 197, 199-201, 223, 230, 231, 238, 254, 255.
Winnebago Lake, 22, 180, 183, 189-196, 206.

Winnebago prophet. *See* White Cloud.
Winnebago Rapids, 196-201.
Winneconne, 22, 164, 179-182.
Wisconsin Central Ry., 144, 160.
Wisconsin Heights, battle of, 254, 266.
Wisconsin River, 17, 21-23, 27, 143-146, 230, 231, 237-293.
Wisconsin River Dells, 23.
Wolf River, 179-183, 185.
Woodman, Wis., 283.
Wright's Ferry, Wis., 27, 289.
Wrightstown, Wis., 213, 214, 220.

YAHARA RIVER. *See* Catfish.

www.ingramcontent.com/pod-product-compliance
Lightning Source LLC
Chambersburg PA
CBHW032049230426
43672CB00009B/1535